THE COMPLETE BOOK OF
PRESSED FLOWERS

THE COMPLETE BOOK OF
PRESSED FLOWERS

PENNY BLACK

Photography by Geoff Dann

DORLING KINDERSLEY   LONDON

To the flowers of our hedgerows, woods and meadows,
the wild and ancient land of Cornwall
and the month of May.

Project Editor Heather Dewhurst
Art Editor Fiona Macmillan

Senior Editor David Lamb
Editorial Director Jackie Douglas
Art Director Roger Bristow

First published in Great Britain in 1988 by
Dorling Kindersley Publishers Limited,
9 Henrietta Street, London WC2E 8PS
First paperback edition 1991
Reprinted 1992, 1993, 1995

Copyright © 1988 Dorling Kindersley Limited, London
Text copyright © 1988 Penny Black

British Library Cataloguing in Publication Data
Black, Penny
The complete book of pressed flowers.
1. Dried flower arrangement 2. Pressed
flower pictures
I. Title
745.92'8   TT880
ISBN 0-86318-746-3

Printed and bound in China by Leefung Asco (Printers) Ltd.
Typeset by Modern Text Typesetters Ltd.
Set in Walbaum on a Monotype Lasercomp.

Contents

~ Introduction ~

My involvement in the art of pressed flowers stems from my lifelong love affair with flowers and gardening. My very first memories are of catching hold of my mother's hand and wandering into a bleak winter garden to look at the little green spears of snowdrops pushing through the frozen soil. Very early on I began to explore the woods, meadows and hedgerows that surrounded our little thatched cottage. From my bedroom window I watched the foxes skirting the woods and fields; I listened to and watched both brown and barn owls; I sat motionless amongst the rabbits; I glimpsed the field- and dormice and occasionally encountered grass snakes and adders. They all fascinated me as much as the flowers, but they were not so easy to find.

Flowers were everywhere and my year began with snowdrops and primroses, followed by an exciting search for the stinking hellebore, and then the daffodils, wood anemones, violets, campions, ragged-robins, bluebells, dog's mercury, orchids and spurge arrived. In those days I picked them all and they were crammed into jam jars with no thought of artistic arrangement. They never lasted long and I yearned to pick more. In our cottage garden I had my own little patch where I grew some of these plants. My mother bought me packets of annual flower seeds and so eagerly did I await their germination that sometimes I dug them up to see what was happening (and I still do

Soft and romantic
(right)
A profusion of summer blooms in shades of pink and lemon is framed within jet beads and rice grains, while a scalloped edging of florets of cow parsley and everlasting flowers provides a pretty finishing touch.

Summer meadow
(right)
The sight of poppies, cornflowers, corncockles and marigolds growing in a meadow is one of the rare beauties of our countryside, and can provide a source of inspiration for your flower pictures.

Abundant garden
(right)
A garden full of flowers can be re-created in a rich and luxuriant flower collage.

"Elizabethan" embroidery
(far right)
The intricate lattice-work of rosebuds, together with the bleached and muted colours of the flowers, give this picture an air of elegance.

that!). With these colourful annuals I made flower dollies with frilled petticoats and bottles of murky looking perfume.

By the time I was about nine I had reclaimed a sizeable patch of the orchard where I crammed a very humble selection of wild and cottage garden plants. I even made a little lawn by cutting the weeds with an old Ransomes lawn-mower. I remember so well the quiet pleasure that it gave me and of sitting there in the gloaming with my cat Puddy, watching the bats and listening to the owls. I lived very close to the cycle of nature and the peace that I found has never left me.

Perfumed Sachets

Surprisingly, as a child I did not press any flowers. In fact I did not start pressing flowers at all until about ten years ago. I had started making and selling perfumed sachets, to earn some money, but with so many people around with the same idea, I felt that to succeed I must come up with something original. Then I had the idea of decorating lace-edged calico sachets with little pressed rosebuds. I thought these would look pretty and unlike other sachets that I had seen. Of course I didn't get it right the first time round but it was not long before these sachets, as you see them in this book, evolved. Over the years I have made thousands of them and they have been my "bread and butter" in the precarious world of selling crafts.

However, my thoughts were always turning to pressed flower collages where I felt that there was tremendous scope. In my mind's eye I could vaguely see what I wanted to do but could never put it into practice. I made plenty of stylized flower pictures but was never happy with them; I wanted to capture the abundance of my garden and the thin collages that I was making did nothing to convey this image.

Just two years ago, in what must have been a moment of lateral inspiration, I made my first jumbled attempt at a "Wild Garden" picture and knew that I was on the right path; I could actually see my garden in it and with a few more attempts I felt confident enough to submit one for an exhibition. It was accepted and that was the beginning of my work as you see it in this book. One idea led to another and I realized that there were endless possibilities.

I now look everywhere for inspiration and ideas for my pictures: in books, paintings and poetry. John Clare's poetry can jog my memory and I am immediately transported to the garden of my childhood:

"The columbine, stone blue or deep night brown,
Their honeycomb-like blossoms hanging down,
Each cottage garden's fond adopted child,
Though heaths still claim them where they still grow wild"

These words conjure up for me a picture thickly encrusted with mosses, columbines and humble cottage garden plants. My "Summer Garland" collage, one of my favourites, was for Ophelia in Shakespeare's *Hamlet*, for dancing around maypoles bedecked with ribbons and for all sorts of romantic notions. The borders around my "Elizabethan Collage" were inspired by and are reminiscent of the richly decorated plasterwork of the sixteenth and seventeenth century manor houses, and I made my "Persian Carpet" collage after looking through a beautifully illustrated book of Omar Khayyam. I am always trying to capture some of the moods and qualities other artists have achieved, such as the strangely ethereal atmosphere of Frances MacIntosh's paintings, the rich and sensuous opulence of Leon Bakst's work and the beautiful ornamental features of Gustav Klimt's pictures.

I hope my book will inspire you to experiment with pressing flowers. Not only will you gain immense satisfaction and pleasure from creating flower pictures, but you will also deepen your knowledge of plants and gardening and develop a greater appreciation for our beautiful countryside.

Rich and resplendent
Purple, red and gold predominate in this luxuriant collage.

Plant Material

*Wherever you live, whether in
the town, in the country, or by the sea,
there is a wide range of flowers,
leaves, mosses, lichens, ferns,
seedheads, and even fruit and vegetables
that you can gather and press for your flower pictures.
The following pages show the different
kinds of plant material available,
but be careful: never pick protected or endangered
plants from the wild.*

~ *Gathering Plant Material* ~

There is a wealth of plant material you can gather for pressing. Don't limit yourself solely to flowers that grow in your garden, but search woodlands and hedgerows, beaches and meadows, where there are lots of unusual things you can press: spiralling stalks; green flowers and silky seedheads; seeds and flowers from trees; and unusual seaweeds. Don't forget ponds and streams either, where you will find water fern, parrot weed and other pond plants. And, of course, grasses and rushes, mosses, lichens and fungi can all be pressed very successfully to create unusual combinations of textures, shapes and colours.

Conserving Plants

When gathering wild plants only pick as much as you need. Remember that it is against the law to pick or uproot any rare wild plant (see page 116 for a list of protected plants). The same applies to the flowers you grow in your garden; there is no point pressing your rarest specimen, and neither should you strip plants of all their blossoms, buds or leaves.

Plant material should be quite dry when you gather it; the early afternoon is the ideal gathering time. Give the flowers a sharp nudge before picking them, if hidden water droplets are jerked out, this means a few more hours of drying are necessary. Select only undamaged, fresh blossoms and leaves, as faded, stale plant material will not improve with pressing. And the sooner you can press your gathered plants, the better the finished results will be.

Flower border
(right)
A summer border is the ideal place to gather flowers for pressing. Here dusky pink scabious, dwarf purple larkspur and oxeye daisies are all ripe for picking.

Shady corner
(below)
Growing wild in this shady patch are rosebay willowherb, crane's-bill and hogweed, all of which press beautifully.

~ Effects of Pressing ~

The most obvious effect of pressing a flower is that it becomes flat and two-dimensional. This immediately alters the whole appearance, shape and size of the plant. Small flowers appear larger when their petals are flattened and spread out, and subtle colours and shapes of petals and leaves become more apparent. You can see different aspects of a flower for the first time, such as the lovely pink flower centres of hellebores and the delicate striping of the undersides of astrantia petals.

Colour Changes

The colours of pressed flowers can also change dramatically. If you compare any freshly picked flower with its pressed counterpart, the two flowers never have exactly the same hue. Many colours acquire more depth and luxury after pressing. Any red flowers that press well, such as roses and anemones, will always become richer and darker and there will also be a touch of blue in their colour. Blue flowers, too, become more intense after pressing. Orange and yellow flowers, such as potentilla, tend to become a shade darker, while green leaves and petals are very variable: some become a richer green whilst some barely change at all. White flowers can often turn the colour of parchment, though very quick drying and pressing can sometimes produce a good white. If you come across some plant material that does not press well and turns brown, don't discard it — instead, mix it with other flowers in a "random" flower collage.

The change in some plants can be startling. Wood cow-wheat and lady's bedstraw, for example, often turn black when pressed and as such can look particularly striking in a flower collage. Another example is Cape marigold, the pink star of the veldt, that turns a beautiful dove grey when pressed. Most red and blue primroses turn a uniform shade of heliotrope, with the exception of the gold-laced and Cowichan polyanthuses which often turn velvety black. If you keep experimenting with pressing different flowers, you will learn which plants press well and produce the most interesting and rewarding results.

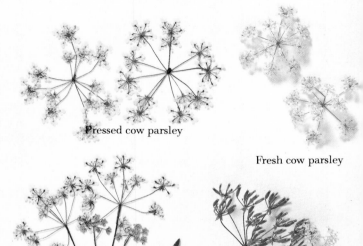

Pressed cow parsley

Fresh cow parsley

Pressed anemones

Fresh anemones

Pressed hydrangea

Pressed rosebuds

Fresh hydrangea

Fresh rosebuds

Pressed wild pansy

Pressed baby's breath

Fresh wild pansy

Fresh baby's breath

• 15 •

～ The Garden ～

The garden is a rich source of colour, providing an abundance of flowers and leaves for pressing all through the year. The striking pinks and reds of old rose blossoms compete with rich purple crane's-bills, scarlet fuchsias and sunny yellow daffodils; while the pale pastel colours of pink and cream anemones, astrantias and Cape marigolds soften and subdue brighter colours.

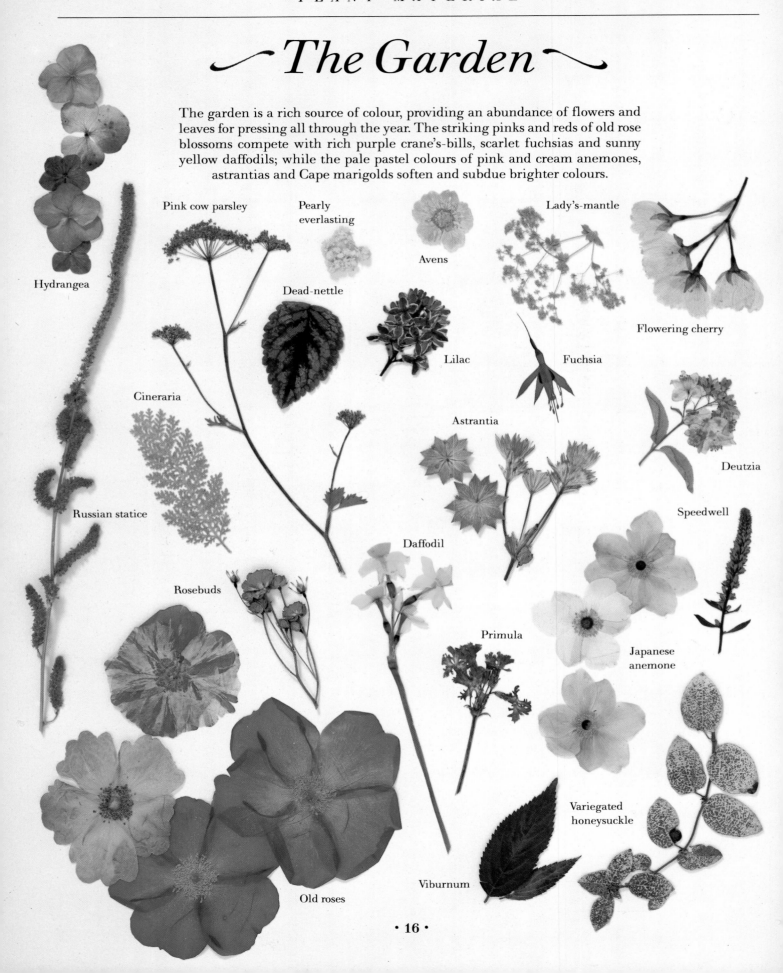

Hydrangea

Pink cow parsley

Pearly everlasting

Avens

Lady's-mantle

Flowering cherry

Dead-nettle

Lilac

Fuchsia

Cineraria

Astrantia

Deutzia

Russian statice

Speedwell

Daffodil

Rosebuds

Primula

Japanese anemone

Variegated honeysuckle

Viburnum

Old roses

Virginia creeper

Crane's-bill

Potentilla

Larkspur

Abutilon

Meadowsweet

Scabious

Borage

Pink meadowsweet

Variegated
goldenrod

Primula

Kolkwitzia

'De Caen'
anemone

Heather

Cape marigold

Loosestrife

Clematis

Allium

Rosebay
willowherb

~ *The Hedgerow* ~

Hedgerows are a rich source of plant material that you can press. There are colourful and pretty celandine and red campion flower-heads, long spiky stems of burnet and pussy willow, and fluffy seedheads of traveller's-joy, while the tiny umbels of cow parsley and hemlock water-dropwort are invaluable for softening edges in your flower pictures.

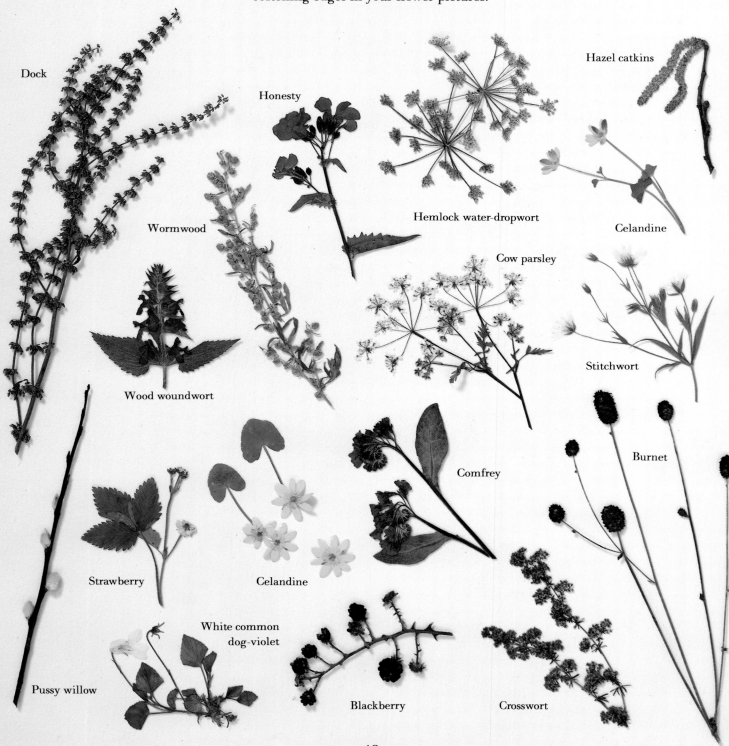

Dock

Honesty

Hazel catkins

Wormwood

Hemlock water-dropwort

Celandine

Cow parsley

Wood woundwort

Stitchwort

Burnet

Comfrey

Strawberry

Celandine

Pussy willow

White common dog-violet

Blackberry

Crosswort

Hop

Yarrow

Climbing fumitory

Common knapweed

Common horsetail

Rat-tailed plantain

Ivy-leaved toadflax

Red campion

Sorrel

Periwinkle

Bitter vetch

Rough chervil

Hazel catkins

Wood sage

Traveller's-joy

Wall fumitory

Rosebay willowherb

~ The Woodland ~

The cool, dappled shade cast by trees in a wood provides a home for many lovely woodland plants. In the spring there are carpets of bluebells and yellow-green spurge, and if you search carefully you will find dainty wood anemones, violets, snowdrops and primroses. Later in the year you can collect all sorts of catkins, berries, seedheads and skeletonized leaves to press.

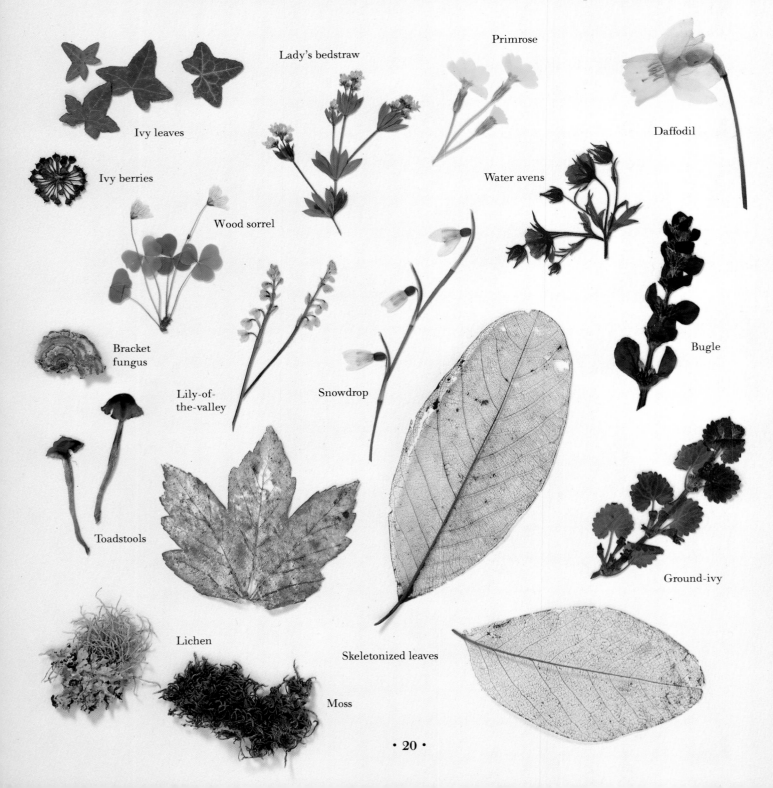

Ivy leaves

Lady's bedstraw

Primrose

Daffodil

Ivy berries

Wood sorrel

Water avens

Bracket fungus

Bugle

Lily-of-the-valley

Snowdrop

Toadstools

Ground-ivy

Lichen

Skeletonized leaves

Moss

Alder catkins

Wood spurge

Spurge

Great wood-rush

Sycamore flowers

Hard shield
fern fronds

Dusky
crane's-bill

Bluebells

White bluebells

Broad
buckler
fern

Maidenhair
spleenwort

Hart's-tongue fern fronds

Wood violet

Wood anemones

Wood forget-
me-not

～ The Seashore ～

If you live by the seashore, you won't be short of plants to press. For, in addition to the many small and colourful flowers that grow by the sea, there is a wide range of seaweed you can collect. With their fascinating spiky and feathery shapes, and their wonderful rich colours of green, red and black, seaweeds are ideal plants for creating atmosphere in a picture.

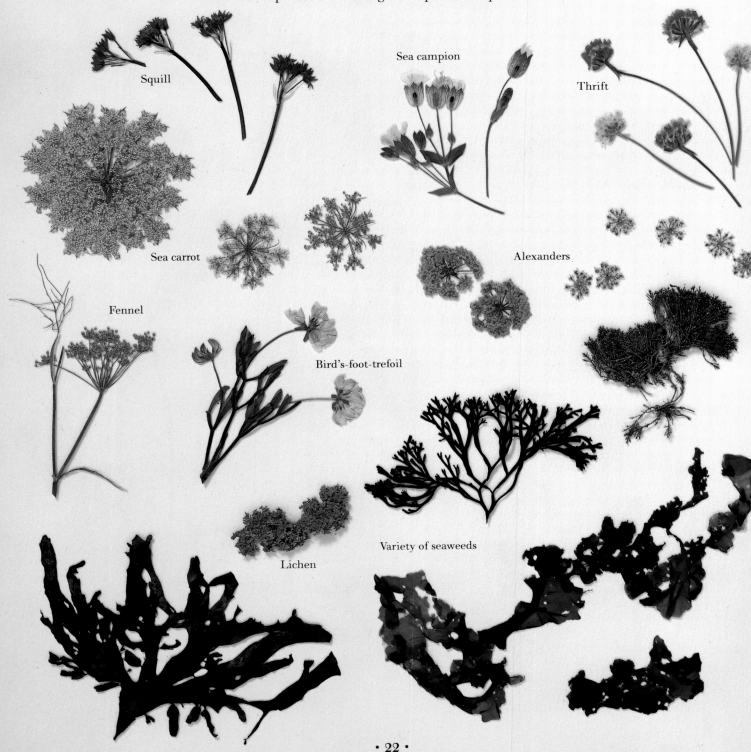

Squill

Sea campion

Thrift

Sea carrot

Alexanders

Fennel

Bird's-foot-trefoil

Lichen

Variety of seaweeds

Variety of seaweeds

Alexanders

~ The Meadow ~

The sight of a wildflower meadow full of colourful flowers immediately fills me with nostalgia. Many of my favourite flowers of childhood thrive in meadow pastures – buttercups, daisies, cowslips and cuckooflowers, all of which press beautifully. But be sensible when picking your flowers; always leave plenty behind to set seed and never pick any rare wild flowers.

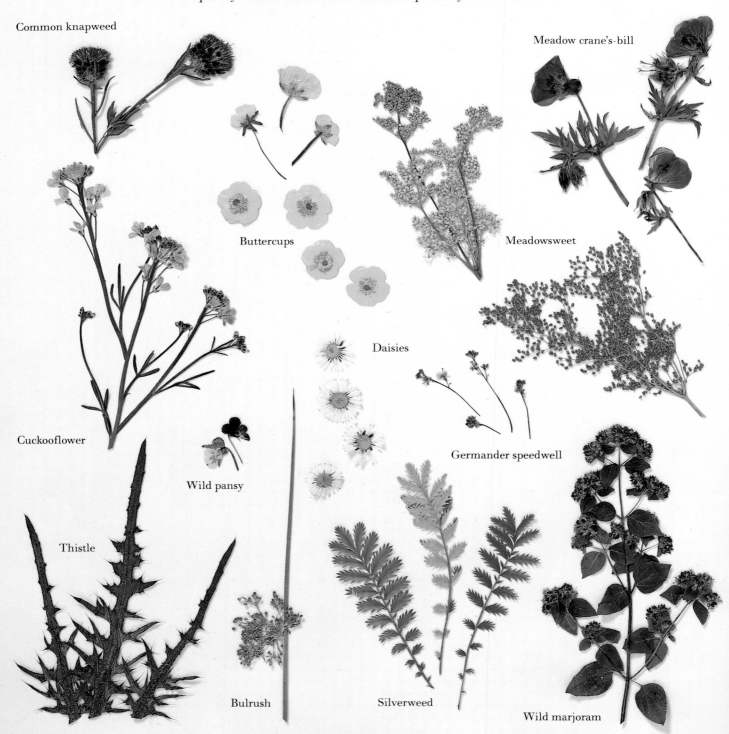

Common knapweed

Meadow crane's-bill

Buttercups

Meadowsweet

Cuckooflower

Daisies

Germander speedwell

Wild pansy

Thistle

Bulrush

Silverweed

Wild marjoram

Cowslips

Red clover

Cow parsley

Bird's-foot-trefoil

Plantain

Sorrel

Marsh-marigold

Various grasses

~Mosses, Lichens & Fungi~

If you search in damp, shady places — on rocks, tree trunks, walls and stream banks — you will find a wealth of mosses and lichens, mushrooms and toadstools, many of which can be used in your flower pictures. Clumps of moss, rich green and springy, or stiff and wiry, and pieces of crusted yellow or greyish-silver lichen add depth and texture, while cross-sections of mushrooms and toadstools provide many unusual shapes and patterns.

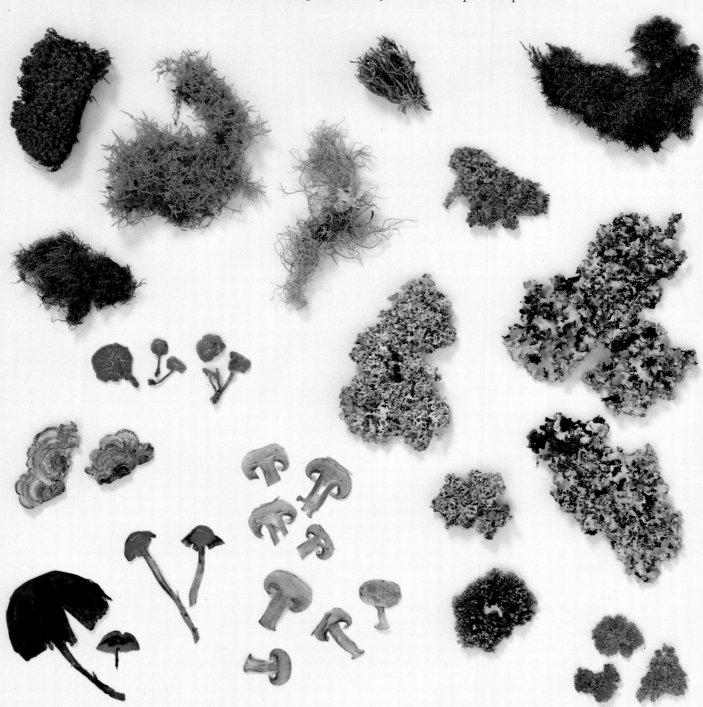

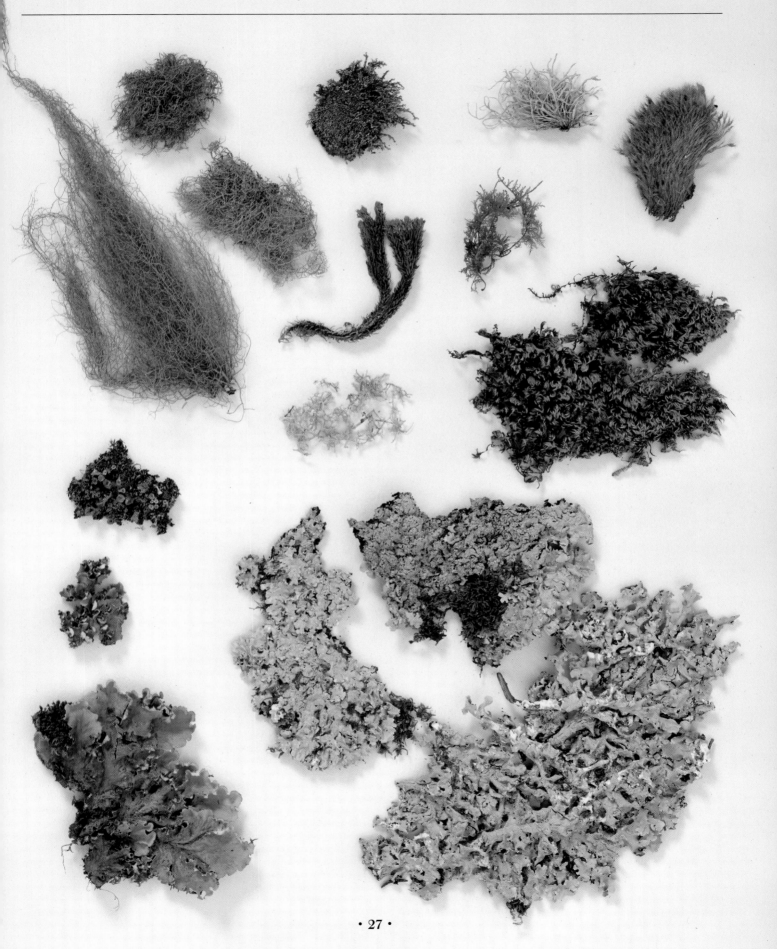

~ Ferns ~

There is a wonderful range of ferns and fern-like leaves you can press and use in your flower pictures, from the light and delicate asparagus fern to the bold and dramatic hart's tongue fern. Ferns are calm and restful, conveying a suggestion of shady glades. The more feathery ferns soften a picture and make pretty lacy patterns, while the thicker and heavier ferns create a bolder image.

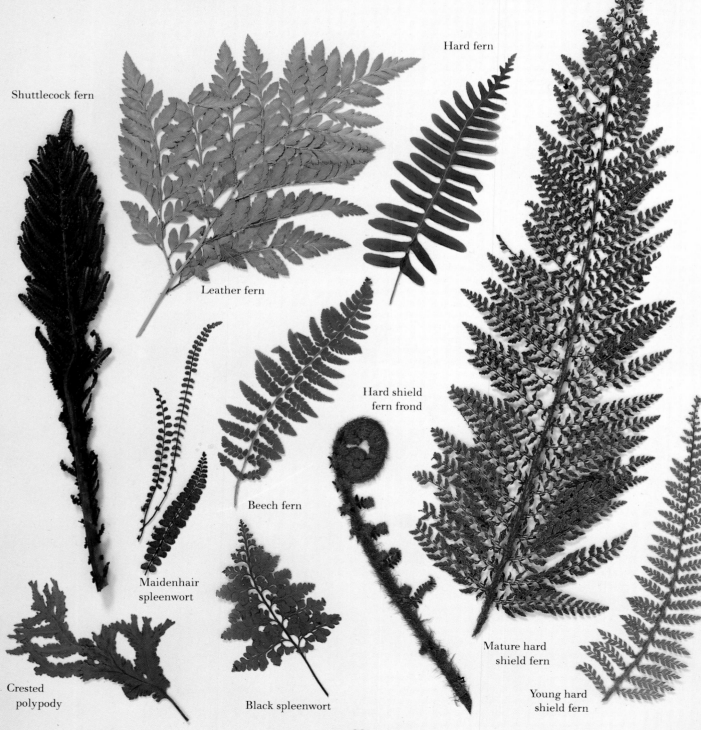

Hard fern

Shuttlecock fern

Leather fern

Hard shield
fern frond

Beech fern

Maidenhair
spleenwort

Crested
polypody

Black spleenwort

Mature hard
shield fern

Young hard
shield fern

Asparagus fern

Bracken

Common polypody

Sweet cicely

Crested buckler fern

Hart's
tongue

Common horsetail

Maidenhair fern

~Seedheads~

There is a tremendous variety of seedheads available for pressing and drying.
Some have fascinating shapes, such as the circular-shaped sea carrot and the
bearded traveller's-joy, while the knobbly clusters of rose hips and blackberries
provide interesting textures. Other seedheads have an unusual beauty, such as
the pearly seed-cases of honesty. As most seedheads are in neutral tones of
brown and green, they can be used in most compositions.

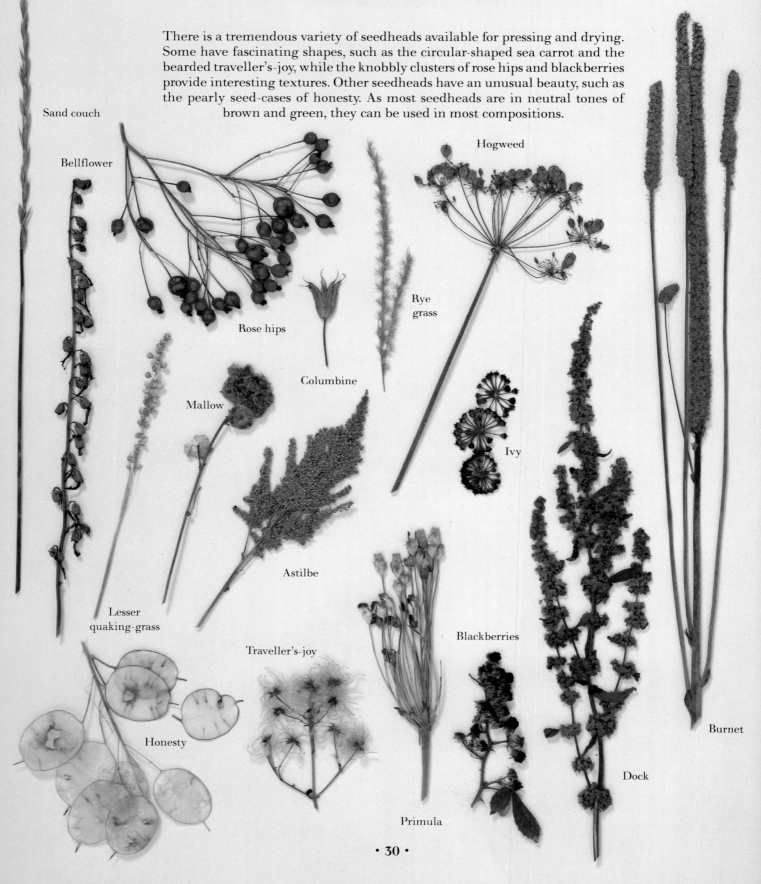

Sand couch

Bellflower

Hogweed

Rose hips

Columbine

Rye
grass

Mallow

Ivy

Astilbe

Lesser
quaking-grass

Traveller's-joy

Blackberries

Honesty

Primula

Dock

Burnet

Columbine

Astilbe

Sea carrot

Yarrow

Sea carrot

Meadow
oat-grass

Jacob's-ladder

Great wood-rush

Meadowsweet

Pennywort

Lavender

Shuttlecock fern

Fruit & Vegetables

From the familiar, homely carrot, to the more exotic kumquat, there is a whole range of fruit and vegetables available for pressing. Red and yellow peppers, strawberries and chilli peppers retain their bright colours, while red cabbage and artichokes make fascinating shapes when pressed. There is also a wonderful array of pulses that can be used to add texture and colour.

Onion rings

Broad bean

Carrot

Strawberries

Watercress

Parsley

Carrot flower

Lychee skin

Alfalfa sprouts

Fennel

Cauliflower

Red lentils

Pumpkin seeds

Aduki beans

Rice

Green lentils

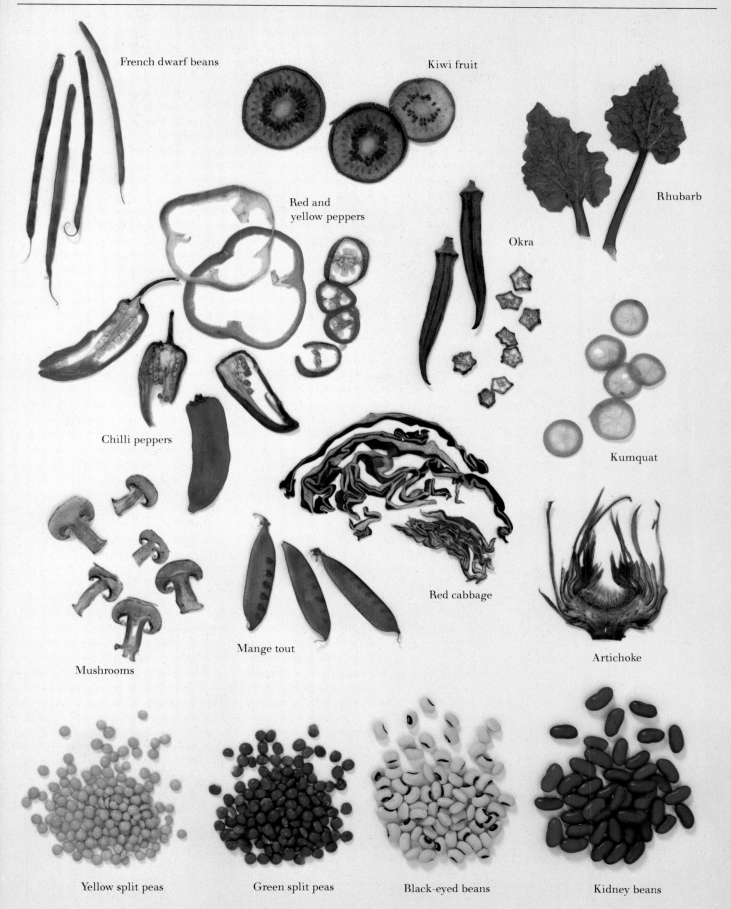

French dwarf beans

Kiwi fruit

Rhubarb

Red and
yellow peppers

Okra

Chilli peppers

Kumquat

Mushrooms

Mange tout

Red cabbage

Artichoke

Yellow split peas

Green split peas

Black-eyed beans

Kidney beans

~ Leaves & Bark ~

Skeletonized leaves are invaluable for my flower pictures and they are not hard to find; I collected the specimens below during a walk through the woods. I use them to form the base layer of my pictures; their intricate veining makes delicate, lacy patterns subduing and softening the colour beneath. Tree bark is useful as its coarse texture adds interest and depth to a picture.

Oak

Holly

Eryngium

Maple

Magnolia

Tree bark

Materials
& Techniques

*The following pages show the
essential tools and equipment you will need
for making pressed flower pictures,
including cutting implements, papers and boards,
fabrics and writing tools.
The techniques to use are simple and straightforward;
with a little practice, you will quickly master
them and be able to set to work
creating your own flower collages.*

∼ Tools & Equipment ∼

The most essential tool I have is an old pair of forceps, with which I handle all my plant material. You may prefer to use tweezers, but I find them a little clumsy.

The other basic items of equipment are: rubber-based glue, orange sticks to apply it, pencils, a rubber and a ruler, French curves to draw round, a sharp knife to cut straight edges, hair spray to fix plant material on completed collages, and a pair of sharp scissors. Many other items are useful but not vital.

The ultimate indulgence, however, would be a room of your own to work in. For years I have worked in the kitchen, on the one and only work surface, surrounded by family and animals, cups of tea and toasted cheese sandwiches. We have all survived quite happily, but what bliss to have a room of one's own!

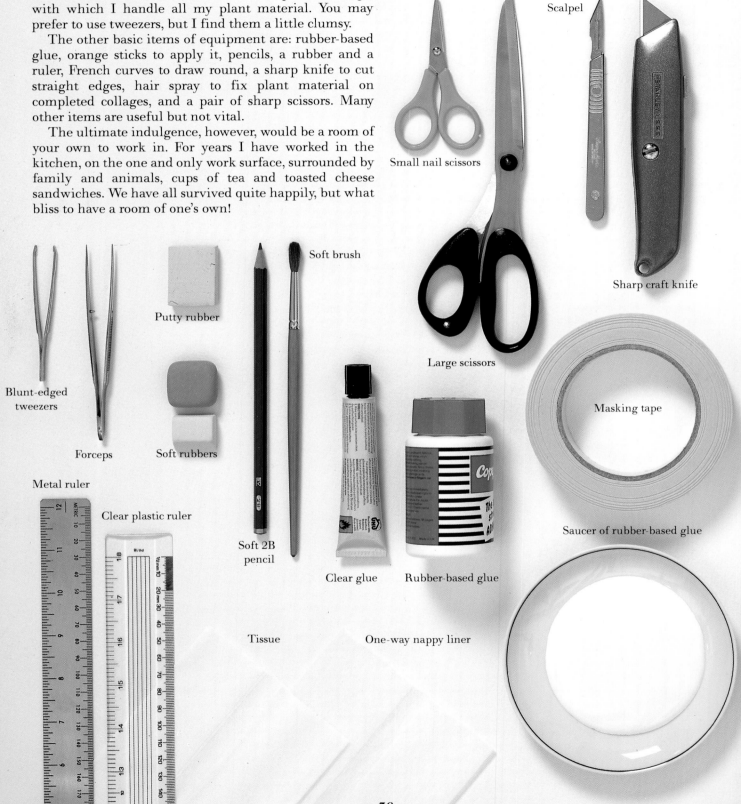

Scalpel

Small nail scissors

Sharp craft knife

Soft brush

Putty rubber

Blunt-edged
tweezers

Forceps

Soft rubbers

Large scissors

Masking tape

Metal ruler

Clear plastic ruler

Soft 2B
pencil

Clear glue

Rubber-based glue

Saucer of rubber-based glue

Tissue

One-way nappy liner

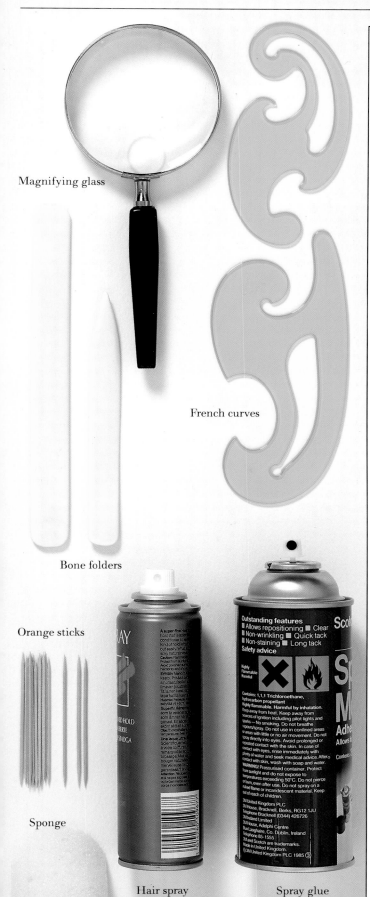

Magnifying glass

French curves

Bone folders

Orange sticks

Sponge

Hair spray

Spray glue

FLOWER PRESSES

Although you may start by using a magazine or heavy book in which to press your flowers and leaves, a flower press does give better results and is essential for those wanting to take the craft seriously. There are several different types and sizes of press available. Two examples are illustrated below.

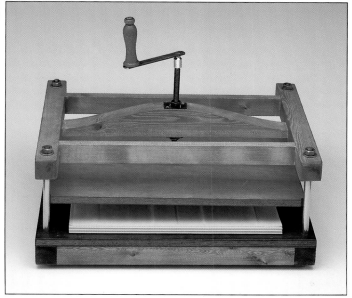

Professional press

This is a heavy-duty professional press which is ideal for those who are serious about flower pressing. With only one central screw it is easy and quick to operate. It can also take a lot of pressure, making it useful for pressing very bulky and textured plant material.

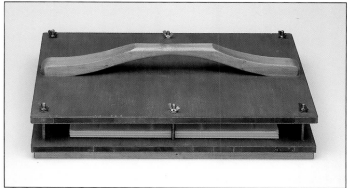

Simple press

This press is lighter and more manageable than the professional press though the pressure it applies is not as great. However, it is perfectly adequate as a general press for flowers and leaves and less textured plant material. It operates by tightening six wing nuts and bolts.

~ *Papers & Boards* ~

The paper you use as a backing for your picture will play an important role in the overall impact that your collage will have. I believe that good quality papers, preferably hand-made, are essential. You will be putting time, thought, and part of yourself into your work, so it deserves to be displayed on beautiful paper.

There are many different types of paper and board you can use, of varying weights, textures and colours. A general rule is to use board or heavyweight paper as backing for larger collages, and lighter weight paper for smaller pictures and cards. Some coloured papers are very pretty and can enhance your flower collage; plain white paper will emphasize the colour and form of your compositions, making their effect more dramatic.

You also have a choice of textures. I always use a heavy and textured paper when backing large and heavily embossed collages. The scrunchy plant materials blend beautifully with the grain of the paper. Papers dyed with and containing such materials as bracken and onion skins are also fun to use. Textured machine-made paper is also available and this serves as an excellent substitute for hand-made paper. More formal compositions, with little texture to them, look better displayed on smooth paper.

Unusual Papers

Continental papers such as Italian marbled paper can make interesting backgrounds. Alternatively, you could try some of the beautiful Japanese papers as backings; these can be very thin, so you may need to back them with a cheaper mediumweight white paper. You can also experiment with flock papers and wallpapers, which can give the impression of brocade or rich velvet.

You will also need absorbent papers for pressing your flower material. I use recycled paper but blotting paper, sugar paper or even newspaper can be just as good.

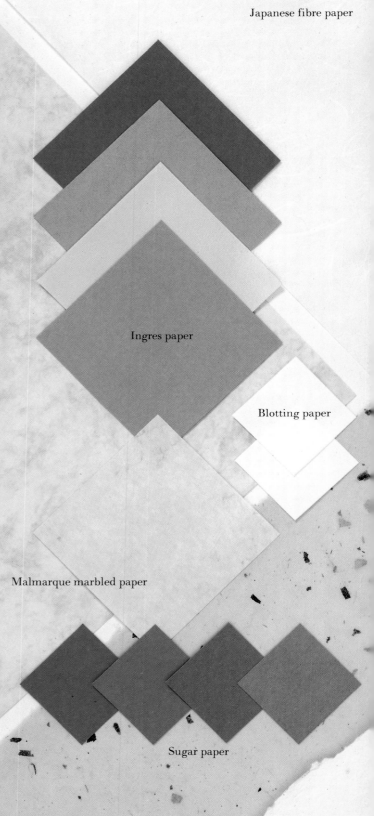

Japanese fibre paper

Ingres paper

Blotting paper

Malmarque marbled paper

Sugar paper

Mounting board

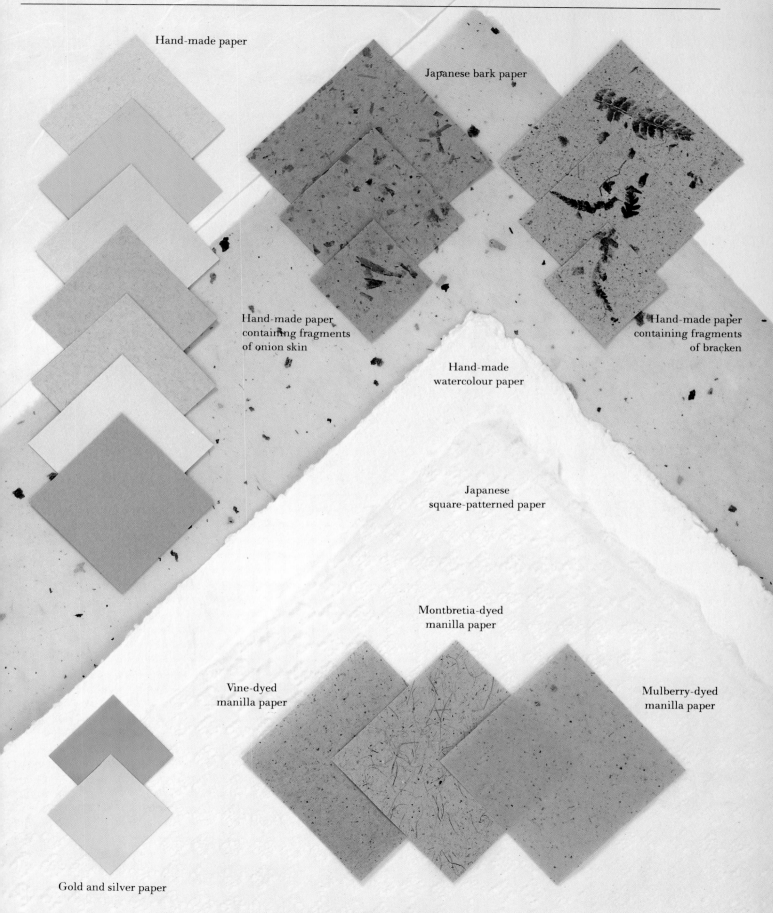

Hand-made paper

Japanese bark paper

Hand-made paper
containing fragments
of onion skin

Hand-made paper
containing fragments
of bracken

Hand-made
watercolour paper

Japanese
square-patterned paper

Montbretia-dyed
manilla paper

Vine-dyed
manilla paper

Mulberry-dyed
manilla paper

Gold and silver paper

~Fabrics~

There is a wide variety of fabric you can use as backings for your pictures, or for making into pillows, sachets or bags. Everyone has a slightly different interpretation as to what is aesthetic. However, there are a few guidelines by which I believe we can all work.

Firstly I recommend that all fabrics used must be natural. Synthetic materials are just not suitable for the pretty, natural image that this work projects. Strong acrylic colours are far too jarring, although it is possible to bleach brightly printed sprigged cottons and chintzes until they are quite pale and look like dimity.

Natural Materials and Dyes

Silks, linens and cottons in neutral shades of coffee, cream, and beige are appropriate for all kinds of pressed flower work. Sew scrim, cotton net or old lace on to unbleached calico for an attractive textured background. Striped cotton ticking, too, can give a modern feel to a brightly coloured flower picture.

You can dye your fabrics with natural dyes, such as lichen, onions, turmeric, marigolds, sloe berries, elderberries and bracken. The results are often quite beautiful, blending subtly with the colours of your pressed flowers. For the detailed techniques of fabric dyeing, see page 108.

Richly coloured silks, brocades and velvets can also be used; they can enrich a flower collage, adding luxury and elegance. Experiment first, to make sure the colours do not overwhelm your flower arrangements.

It is a good idea to back most fabrics with interfacing, as this gives the fabric body and prevents creasing. Alternatively, you can back your fabric with lightweight synthetic wadding for a soft and slightly quilted effect. This can look very pretty for lace pillows and cushions.

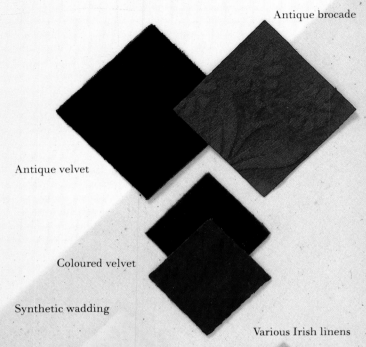

Antique brocade

Antique velvet

Coloured velvet

Synthetic wadding

Various Irish linens

Interfacing

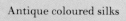

Antique coloured silks

Lichen-dyed silk (left)
and undyed silk

Indian silk

Water-silk taffeta

Scrim

Irish linen

Victorian silk taffeta

Bleached and unbleached cotton prints

Ecclesiastical silks

Calico

Cotton ticking

Lace trimmings

Antique lace

~Making a Picture~

When you first attempt to make a flower picture, allow yourself plenty of time, plenty of space and have everything to hand: glue, card, orange sticks, scissors, plus, of course, lots of pressed plant material. A good idea is to group your pressed flowers according to shape, size or colour, so you don't have to spend a lot of time sifting through a mass of pressed flowers each time you want to glue a specimen on your picture.

It may take you a while to get used to handling forceps or tweezers and you may damage the odd flower or stalk as a result. But don't worry – you will soon gain confidence.

The basic instructions for making a flower picture are outlined below. Once you have mastered the different techniques involved and can handle the plant material with ease, you can begin to experiment and create your own individual flower pictures.

A successful picture is one that is pleasing to look at and does not offend the eye. So it should have a balance both in its composition and in its use of colour. I also think a picture should be *interesting* to look at, so make use of all the varying textures and shapes of plant material that are available in your flower picture.

THE BASIC STEPS

1 Cut out the backing card. Brush rubber-based glue over it. Carefully position the skeletonized leaves on the glued card, starting from centre top.

2 Trim the leaves where they overlap the card. Carefully dip moss and lichen into a saucer of rubber-based glue and then position them on the picture.

3 Hold delicate blossoms with forceps. Dab glue on the back of each flower-centre with an orange stick. Carefully place the flowers in position.

4 Glue sprays of flowers on to the moss. Dab glue on to small leaves with an orange stick and press them gently in position around the edges of the card. Stick small blossoms on the picture.

5 Before completing the picture, turn it on to its reverse side and, holding it gently with one hand, and resting the picture on the table, trim the bottom edge with sharp scissors.

6 Dab glue on to the lower third of long flower stalks with an orange stick. Then, using forceps, tuck the stalks behind flowers and pads of moss. These will complete your flower picture.

The finished picture
*With its delicate combination of muted russets and greens, the
collage has a mellow, autumnal air.*

Pens & Inks

As a finishing touch to your flower picture, you may like to add your name and the date, or the title of your picture. Remember to use as fine a pen as possible. I find that a fine technical drawing pen is best for writing on paper and a fine polyacetate-tipped pen for writing on fabric. You could also use a fine-nibbed italic pen or a mapping pen, which you can dip into gold leaf paint or water-soluble ink. Inks are available in a variety of colours; you only need a few basic colours from which you can then mix your own shades.

For drawing surrounds to pictures, use thicker felt-tipped pens, experimenting with the many colours available. Pastel crayons are also very useful; use them to create beautiful backgrounds in soft colours that will blend well with the natural colours of your flowers.

Soft lead pencil

Fine technical drawing pen

Very fine polyacetate-tipped pens

Propelling pencil

Various nibs

Nib reservoir

Fine mapping pen

Pastel crayons

Fine gold marker pen

Gold leaf paint

Water-soluble inks

Italic pen

Water-based felt-tipped pens

Broad silver marker pen

Spirit-based marker pens

Drawing inks

Turkey feather quill pen

Composition, Colour & Texture

*The following pages show you how to
plan your flower pictures: what composition
style to choose, which colours to use,
and how to combine different textures.
You can make a rich, luxuriant
composition in majestic tones of red
and purple, or a soft, romantic picture
using pastel colours and feathery textures.
These pages provide the guide,
but the key is to experiment.*

~Composition~

The composition of your flower pictures is both the overall form of the arrangement as well as the way you combine and group specimens in the arrangement.

Some overall forms are conventional and might inspire you: circular or oval garlands, bouquets and posies, friezes or the repetitive designs of borders. Then there is the form that botanists use to record their specimens with lots of space between them. All of these will bear every interpretation your imagination can come up with. And there is an infinite number of free-form collages to create where the overall composition is random. You might even choose to make compositions that combine forms, a bouquet with a border for example.

Developing a Style

How you combine flowers and other plant material is a matter of your own taste in shape and colour. This is the part of making pressed flower pictures that allows your own style to grow and flourish. You will remember successful combinations and use them again. If you decide on a lush approach, include any material that is aesthetically pleasing to you, mingling sprays, single blossoms, leaves, lichens and mosses. There need be no uniformity — a haphazard arrangement is both natural and charming. With such pictures, I like to create a feeling of depth, using tall spindly specimens in the foreground to partially obscure "distant" blooms.

Garland card
(top right)
An oval garland of roses featuring the exquisite 'Veilchenblau' rose at centre top.

Flower basket
(far right)
This traditional composition is given a modern look against cotton ticking.

Lush frieze *(right)*
This short frieze is a rich profusion of mingled wild and garden flowers, all picked during early summer.

Rich & Luxuriant

There is tremendous scope for creating rich and luxuriant flower pictures. Just let your imagination have free rein and experiment with all the different flowers, leaves, spikes and sprays that are available. Combine different colours, textures and shapes together. Dark reds, bright, glowing yellows and rich greens create a lush impression while the different textures of coarse lichens, spiky long-stemmed plants and smooth soft blooms add interest and variety to the collage. You can make a lush tapestry of blooms and leaves, arranged in a loose, abstract design, each corner providing a feast for the eyes; or you can build an overflowing densely packed picture crammed with blossoms, lichens and tall spindly stems.

The first step is to make a base layer of skeletonized leaves which you might already have sprayed a different colour. Then display your selected combination of plant material over this layer, perhaps in a random, abstract fashion, pads of moss overlapping large rose blooms, feathery ferns and florets of sea carrot decorating the edges, sprays of deutzia and hydrangea partially shrouding larger blooms. For a stunning impact you could arrange bold slabs of colour together, a mass of dark red roses, for example, and then offset these with paler colours, to create contrast. For a distinctive finishing touch, scatter shells and beads throughout the collage adding glamour, sparkle and a hint of luxury.

Random collage *(right)*
A haphazard arrangement of colourful blossoms overlapping with mosses, leaves and sprays is set against a lacy background of skeletonized leaves.

Moonlight garden *(far right)*
Cool tones of silver, grey and cream combine in this picture to produce a rich yet subtle effect. Jet and crystal beads add a hint of opulence.

Simple & Botanical

My simple and botanical compositions are inspired by the plant drawings found in sixteenth and seventeenth century herbals. The naive simplicity of these drawings is most attractive; single specimen plants, often including the roots, were meticulously drawn in a rather stylized form. Isolated flower-heads and seed capsules were frequently displayed separately alongside the parent plant, and each part was labelled individually.

These pictures originally served a purely instructive purpose but have since come to be regarded as very decorative. It is with this latter purpose in mind that I have developed my botanical style of composition.

Single Specimens

Making a picture from a single pressed flower specimen is one of the easiest to do and a good way to build up your confidence in creating flower pictures. Successful botanical compositions are clear, simple and neat, with lots of white background visible.

You can use any specimen of plant you like; pretty, small plants such as chamomile, threepenny-bit roses and buttercups are good for small cards, but if you are making a larger picture, you could use larger specimens or groups of plants, such as a collection of cottage garden plants, or a group of sweet-smelling herbs.

Taking the picture a stage further, you could make a border of rosebuds or create a pale colour-washed border with no ornamentation at all. For the more elaborate borders, you could make an abstract collage of flowers. Inspiration and ideas can be gleaned from the richly illuminated pages of old herbals.

Botanical Herbal

In my Elizabethan picture, shown opposite, I have displayed a variety of plants that would have been grown in Elizabethan times: old damask roses, ferns, astrantias, scabious, cuckooflowers and lungwort. I gathered most of them from my own garden and then pressed them, the little ferns complete with their roots. Hemlock water-dropwort, cuckooflowers and the old roses are all steeped in herbal lore and have been painted and written about for hundreds of years. Sweetly scented bergamot and the little astrantias are also very old plants. The specimen plants are surrounded by a beautifully coloured border collage, a rich and luxuriant style of composition that contrasts well with the simple specimen plants. The arched rectangle has been edged with little rosebuds in the ornamental fashion of the old herbals.

There are many other themes you can develop and you only need to look to nature for your inspiration.

Cottage garden herbs
A collection of cottage garden herbs are displayed simply within a decorative border.

Rosebud card
The sparse arrangement of tiny rosebuds and a rose leaf inside a square border give this card a quiet elegance.

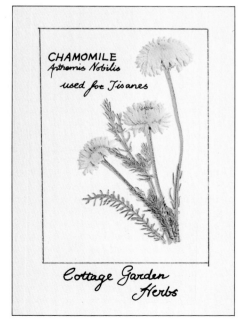

Botanical card
The very starkness of this card adds charm to the lovely specimen of double chamomile.

Elizabethan herbal
*A simple display of old-fashioned Elizabethan-style flowers
is enriched by a colourful, decorative border,
made in a contrasting style of composition.*

Soft & Romantic

The soft and romantic style of composition is ideally suited to pressed flowers. With the smooth curving shapes, soft, feathery textures and pretty pastel colours of many pressed flowers and leaves, you are halfway there. My own interpretation of the soft and romantic style is of classical swags, festoons, garlands and borders of flowers threaded through with silk ribbons and edged with lace trimmings. You will not have to look to the natural world for inspiration. Instead an appreciation of the ornamental and decorative arts is essential. Ceramic designs, textiles and embroidery can all give you inspiration for this delicate and expressive form of collage.

The Techniques

There is a certain discipline involved in this style of composition; the naturalistic curves and flowing sweeps are all carefully planned so that the balance and proportions of the picture are accurate. Instead of superimposing plant material haphazardly, one piece on top of another, the background should always show through. Each blossom, leaf, spray or petal should be thoughtfully positioned, with an eye to the overall shape of the arrangement. Any plant material that has a natural curve to it is very easy to place, such as the drooping flower-heads of water avens and the gently curving fern fronds. Pastel coloured rose and potentilla blooms and pale astrantia flower-heads can form the outlines of the

swag or garland, and other smaller flowers, such as rosebuds, elder flowers, florets of water dropwort, cow parsley and sea carrot, can fill the gaps. Trailing bows of silk ribbon can be woven through your flowers and lace can be used to edge your picture.

Garlands and Swags

Soft and romantic compositions work well on any scale, whether they be small greetings cards or large pictures for your wall. A garland arrangement can look very pretty on a card. Use the tiniest blooms — roses, potentilla and hydrangea — and edge them with creamy florets of sea carrot and delicate sprays of meadowsweet.

For larger garlands, you can use larger, more dominant blooms without the risk of them overpowering the collage. You can also make the garland denser, perhaps padded out with moss and greater quantities of blossoms. Create pretty lacy edges with sprays of baby's breath, great wood-rush, and frills of cow parsley.

The gentle drooping curves of a pressed flower swag seem to flow naturally and have an air of elegance. Swags, festoons and drapes can be as long as you like, depending on the area you have to hang them. Soft, smooth shapes look best and it adds to the formality if the "loops" of flowers balance each other in content as well as style. Small fern fronds look pretty drooping out of the swag while ivy leaves can be used to form an apex.

Romantic lace garland (above)
This pretty garland of summer flowers is bordered with antique lace for a special effect.

A simple charm (above left)
A garland of roses, interwoven with a golden silk ribbon, is edged with soft florets of sea carrot and meadowsweet.

Pressed flower swag (left)
The elegant sweeping curves of ivy leaves and richly coloured blossoms are softened by gently trailing fern fronds to form a swag.

~Colour~

The colours you use in your flower picture form an important part of its composition and will determine the overall impact of the design. Bright and vibrant colours, such as reds and yellows, create a strong image and immediately catch one's eye; muted pastel colours convey a feeling of delicacy and softness; while the dark, sombre shades of brown and grey and deep green add a touch of drama and moodiness.

A successful picture will depend upon your appreciation of colour. Some people have an instinctive understanding and feel for colour, but this can also come with experience. For those who are unsure about mixing colours together, a basic knowledge of the theory of colour provides a good starting point.

The Theory of Colour

The colours of the spectrum, from red through to violet, can form a complete circle, each colour progressing to the next. This circle is known as the colour wheel, and is shown here made from a selection of pressed flowers.

The three primary colours — red, yellow and blue — are the strongest colours in the spectrum and you should use these with care, as they can easily dominate and

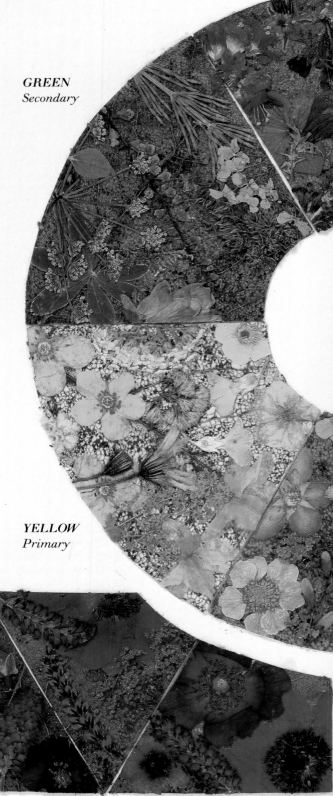

GREEN
Secondary

YELLOW
Primary

The colour wheel (right)
All the colours of the spectrum are shown in this colour wheel of pressed flowers. The three primary colours of red, yellow and blue and the three secondary colours of orange, green and violet can be combined in complementary or contrasting colour schemes within your picture.

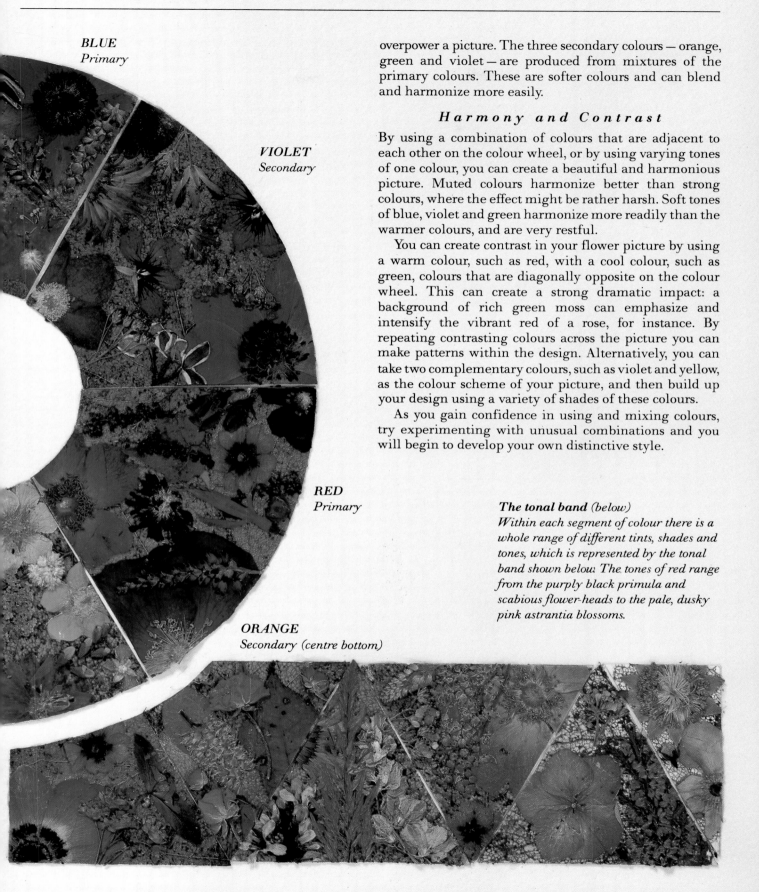

BLUE
Primary

VIOLET
Secondary

RED
Primary

ORANGE
Secondary (centre bottom)

overpower a picture. The three secondary colours — orange, green and violet — are produced from mixtures of the primary colours. These are softer colours and can blend and harmonize more easily.

Harmony and Contrast

By using a combination of colours that are adjacent to each other on the colour wheel, or by using varying tones of one colour, you can create a beautiful and harmonious picture. Muted colours harmonize better than strong colours, where the effect might be rather harsh. Soft tones of blue, violet and green harmonize more readily than the warmer colours, and are very restful.

You can create contrast in your flower picture by using a warm colour, such as red, with a cool colour, such as green, colours that are diagonally opposite on the colour wheel. This can create a strong dramatic impact: a background of rich green moss can emphasize and intensify the vibrant red of a rose, for instance. By repeating contrasting colours across the picture you can make patterns within the design. Alternatively, you can take two complementary colours, such as violet and yellow, as the colour scheme of your picture, and then build up your design using a variety of shades of these colours.

As you gain confidence in using and mixing colours, try experimenting with unusual combinations and you will begin to develop your own distinctive style.

The tonal band *(below)*
Within each segment of colour there is a whole range of different tints, shades and tones, which is represented by the tonal band shown below. The tones of red range from the purply black primula and scabious flower-heads to the pale, dusky pink astrantia blossoms.

~ Colour & Mood ~

A love of flowers, their many colours and the different moods they can evoke, are what my collages are all about. When flowers are pressed, their colours can change quite dramatically, becoming either more intense, or softer and more subdued. To convey a certain atmosphere or mood through your collage, you should combine your colours carefully, decide which colour you want to dominate the collage and what colour you want to use as a background.

Moods to Create

Colours can be rich and vibrant, creating a warm, mellow mood. You can combine the majestic red of old roses, the luscious pinks of astilbe and speedwell and the rich greens of moss and ferns for a warm, relaxing picture, and use a warm red or pink background to emphasize the mood.

For a picture with a more soothing and restful atmosphere, use paler, more subdued coloured blooms, such as potentilla, hydrangea and elder blossoms, in shades of white, cream, pink and yellow. Contrast these with fresh green fern fronds for a cooling effect.

To create a lively, theatrical picture, use bold contrasting colours such as bright yellows and purples, and add startling extras such as glitter and sequins, or gold and silver paint. For a sunny cheerful picture without the glitter, use a combination of bright oranges, yellows and reds — montbretia, potentilla and roses, for example.

Alternatively, convey an atmosphere of dreaminess and romance using the soft colours of cream, pink and baby blue. Cow parsley, sprays of meadowsweet, hydrangea blooms and tiny threepenny-bit roses can all be used, and add frills of lace and silk bows for a finishing touch.

Try experimenting with different combinations of colours to suit your mood. There are really no hard and fast rules: everything depends upon individual taste.

Rich red collage
(right)
The strong reds and greens of the composition are enhanced by the sumptuous red backing of antique brocade to give a warm mellow atmosphere.

Magical wilderness
(right)
The tones of platinum grey, jet black and purple contrast strongly with pink and crimson blossoms to create an ethereal and sombre mood.

~ Changing Colour ~

Pressed flowers often have a depth of colour and feel of luxury that no fresh flowers can equal, such as the beautiful and velvety crimson old roses. However, it can be fun sometimes to change or enhance these colours to produce a more dramatic and theatrical flower picture.

I had great fun making the picture opposite. All the plant material in it, with the exception of the white everlasting flowers, has been sprayed with different coloured paint — yellow, red, black, green, silver and gold.

The bold red and yellow roses, anemones and hydrangea blooms throw into sharp relief the pure white everlasting flowers with their sunny yellow centres, while a hint of drama is added with the impressive, black spikes of Scots lovage and loosestrife. I sprayed the moss a richer green and the pink cow parsley a deeper pink, while the moss basket was changed to gold.

BEFORE & AFTER COLOURING

Elder

Scots lovage

Anemone

Sea carrot

Skeletonized leaves

Loosestrife

Edwardian basket
With the addition of coloured spray paint, this simple basket of summer blooms has become a lavish, theatrical display.

~Using Background Washes~

I really enjoy using and experimenting with background washes. They can change completely the impact and message that a picture has to convey. Pastel colour washes soften a cold white background; I often use a colour wash of palest pink as a background for lovely old roses.

Colours with far more depth can also be used as background washes, and then covered with skeletonized leaves. Gaudy and vibrant washes become softer and more subtle with the fine tracery of leaves covering them. Reds, purples, deep blues and greens, harsh acid yellows, oranges and shocking pinks can all look most effective. For a really dramatic and sumptuous composition, leave the vibrant colour-washed background uncovered, but balance this with dramatic plant material in the collage. Often the most unlikely colour combinations, that probably break all the rules, will look beautiful.

Applying a Wash

It is a good idea to experiment with the colours before you actually apply the wash, in case the tone is too intense or too pale. The first step is to dampen the paper by brushing water over it with a large brush or sponge. This makes the wash easier to apply. Mix a generous amount of water with some watercolour paint in a saucer. Load your brush with paint from the saucer and make a brushstroke right across the top of the paper from left to right and then back again. Dip your brush in the saucer again and repeat the process down the paper. To achieve the effect of graduated colour, keep adding water to the saucer of paint, to lighten the tone, and keep the brushstrokes fluid and smooth, so that the colour blends in.

When using the more vibrant colours, particularly if they are to be covered with skeletonized leaves, mix the paint with Chinese White watercolour paint and only a little water. This adds depth and opaqueness to the wash.

A theatrical effect (right)
The background colours of deep purple, blue and pink echo the shades of the anemone blossoms to produce a rich "Persian carpet" collage.

Nylon square-edged brush

Nylon
watercolour brush

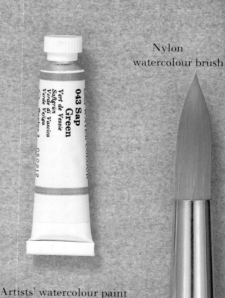

Artists' watercolour paint

Sponge

~Texture~

Smooth

There is a wealth of smooth plant material you can use in your flower pictures, from velvety rose petals and glossy ivy leaves to tiny, delicate hydrangea blooms. Smooth textured petals and leaves contrast well with the coarser, chunkier plant material shown opposite. Try edging silky rose blooms with clumps of moss and lichen, to give depth and interest to the picture.

The large, soft flower-heads of old roses and anemones can be used to form the focal point of a collage. They will dictate a colour scheme, around which the rest of the collage can be created. Care must be taken in the pressing of smooth plant material, however, as it will be very closely scrutinized. Smaller flowers, such as florets of hydrangea and yarrow add a touch of subtlety to a picture. They can be used to soften the hard edges of larger blooms and to emphasize a dominant feature. Small sprays can also be used as a decorative finishing touch.

Forget-me-not

Potentilla

Virginia creeper

Deutzia

Clematis

Honesty

Cuckooflower

Flowering cherry

'De Caen' anemone

Black spleenwort

Japanese anemone

Primula

Ivy

Hydrangea

Yarrow

Crane's-bill

Old rose

Coarse

Coarse plant material plays a very important role in the composition of my flower pictures, producing a three-dimensional effect, casting shadows and creating depth and interest. But don't overdo the coarse elements in a picture or the result will be too heavy. Instead, mix them with smooth blossoms and leaves for contrast.

There is a wide variety of textured plant material that you can use, in all shapes and sizes and with varying levels of coarseness. There are tall and brittle thistles and grasses, knobbly twigs of pussy willow and witch hazel, heavily laden sprays of catkins and hips, thick springy clumps of moss and marvellously lumpy lichens. Even pressed strawberries, green loganberries, raspberries, blackcurrants and blackberries are all effective, providing an interesting splash of colour as well as unusual texture.

It is useful to keep a ready supply of coarse plant material in fairly neutral colours. Dark brown alder catkins, rich green moss and the pretty pinkish quaking-grass are good examples. This material can then be used to add texture in any composition, without confusing the colour scheme.

Eryngium

Alder catkins

Monk's-hood

Meadow oat-grass

Knapweed

Roses

Witch hazel

Rose hips

Lesser quaking-grass

Hop

Blackberry

Moss

Ivy berries

Lichen

Bark

Pussy willow

Feathery

Feathery plant material has a soothing influence in a flower picture, balancing the effect of the heavy coarse elements and the bright colourful blossoms, and contrasting with sharp and spiky plants.

Delicate sprays of baby's breath and lady's-mantle can be arranged around large, brightly coloured flowers, softening their impact and perhaps correcting a jarring note. The tiny brown flower-heads of great wood-rush can provide a pretty lacy edging around bold shapes, while the pale creamy umbels of sea carrot and cow parsley break up a sharp edge.

The gently tapering leaves of sweet cicely and asparagus fern can shroud and mist bold shapes, subtly altering colours and adding a calming influence. The fluffy beards of traveller's-joy and soft astilbe flower-heads add an intriguing tactile quality to a flower picture.

The colours of feathery sprays and blossoms tend to be pale and neutral, which also adds to their soothing effect. Pale green hemlock water-dropwort and lady's-mantle, creamy yellow sea carrot and elder flowers and the soft white blossoms of baby's breath can be used liberally in most compositions, without affecting the colour scheme.

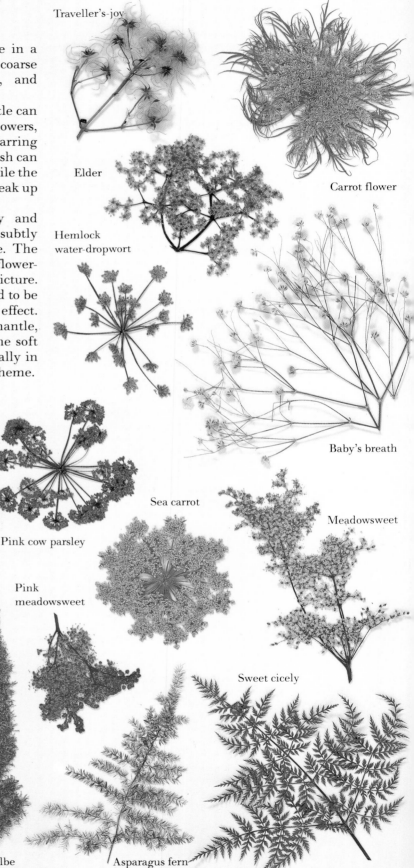

Traveller's-joy

Elder

Carrot flower

Hemlock water-dropwort

Baby's breath

Lady's-mantle

Pink cow parsley

Sea carrot

Meadowsweet

Pink meadowsweet

Allium

Sweet cicely

Great wood-rush

Astilbe

Asparagus fern

Spiky

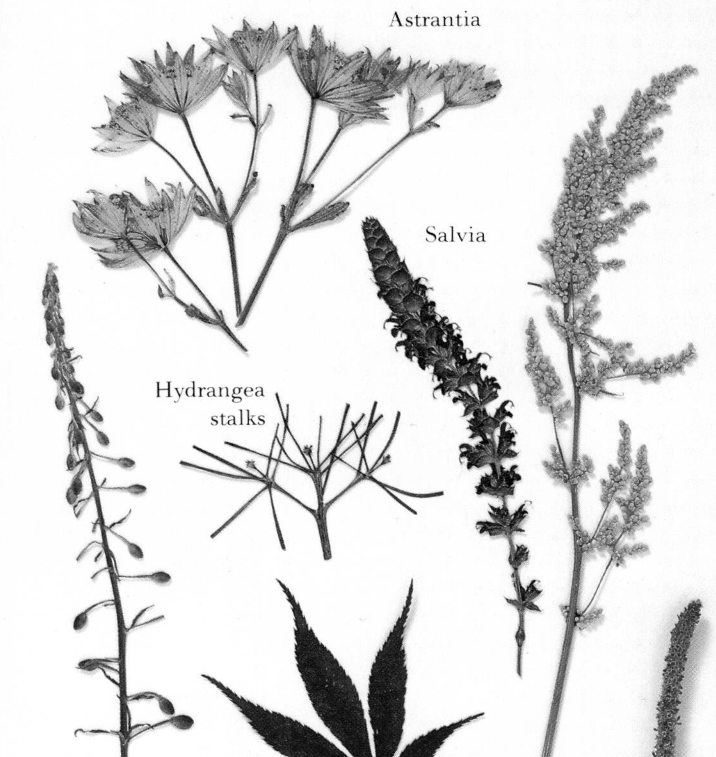

Astrantia

Salvia

Hydrangea
stalks

Maple

Japanese
cedar

Burnet

Mugwort

Phormium

Russian
statice

Scabious

Rosebay
willowherb

Loosestrife

Sea-holly

Corkscrew
rush

Astilbe

Speedwell

Cape marigold

Spiky plant material adds architectural interest to a flower picture and can bring it to life. Tall vertical spikes of rosebay willowherb, phormium and burnet can look quite dramatic, contrasting with the different textures of small, soft blooms and with the delicate feathery leaves and flowers shown opposite.

There are many interesting shapes of spiky material that you can use, ranging from the long, pointed stems of speedwell and loosestrife to the spiny star-shaped calyx of sea-holly flowers. There are also sharply toothed maple leaves, spiralling corkscrew rushes, spiky hydrangea stalks, and pointed astrantia petals, all of which add interest to a picture.

Spiky plant material is often intensely coloured, such as the lovely pinkish-red Russian statice, which could be used as the striking centrepiece of a picture.

Care must be taken when positioning spiky stalks and blossoms in your flower picture in case you crowd it with long vertical stripes. It is a good idea to look at a high summer border in your garden to see the interaction between vertical and horizontal plants; you may be able to incorporate these ideas in your design.

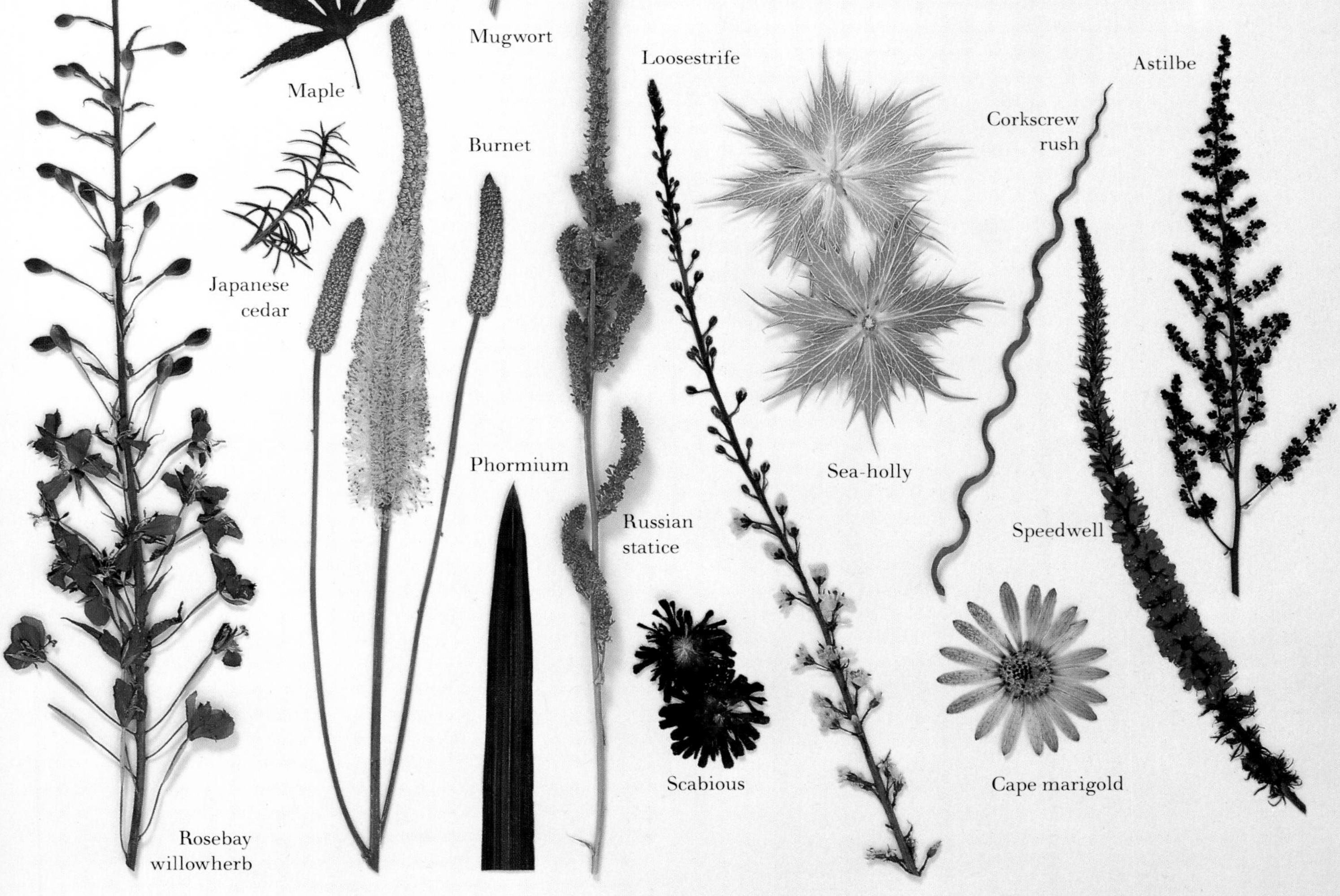

Non-Flower Material

Having magpie tendencies is a great advantage when it comes to collecting non-flower material for my flower pictures. Over the years I have amassed a veritable horde of beads, lace trimmings, ribbons, shells, sea glass, sequins, silk and satin threads, semi-precious stones, buttons, fossils and other intriguing bits and bobs. If you enjoy embroidery and dressmaking, you are bound to have many oddments you can use, otherwise you can experiment with any bric-a-brac you have.

There are lots of imaginative ways of using non-flower material in your flower pictures, all of which add interest, sparkle and fun. You can glue sequins or beads in flower centres, thread delicate silk ribbons through nosegays and garlands, and you can even make butterflies and moths from silky threads, sequins and beads, to add an element of surprise to a picture. Little shells can nestle amongst mosses and lichens, fossils and unusual pieces of sea glass can be arranged at the base of your picture, and glitter can be sprinkled amongst the foliage. Then there are seeds and spices that you could arrange in haphazard groups, as edgings or even as intriguing garnishes. The possibilities are endless, limited only by your imagination.

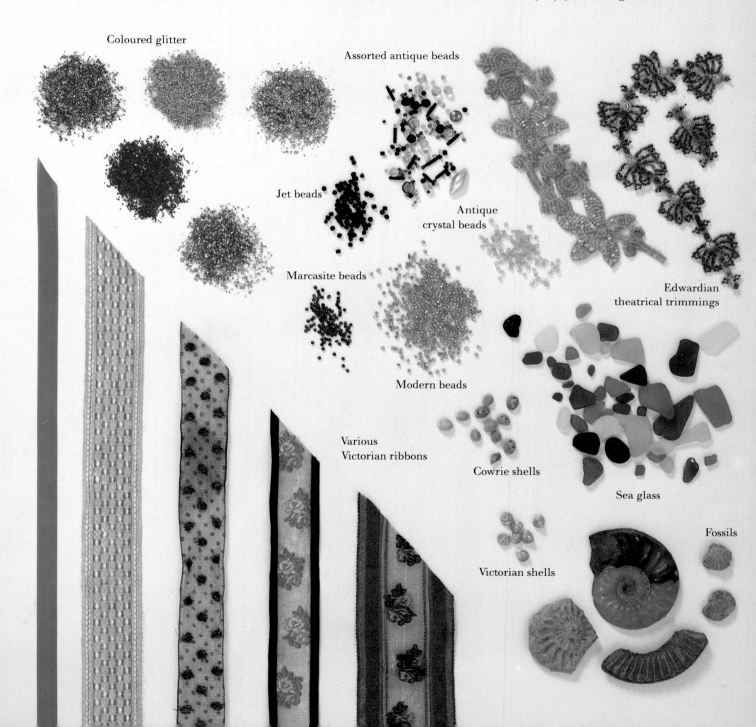

Coloured glitter

Assorted antique beads

Jet beads

Antique crystal beads

Edwardian theatrical trimmings

Marcasite beads

Modern beads

Various Victorian ribbons

Cowrie shells

Sea glass

Victorian shells

Fossils

Flower
Projects

This section illustrates many different
flower projects you can make with
pressed flowers and other plant material.
From a lush wild garden collage
to a romantic summer garland, from a cheerful
kitchen poster to a perfumed lace sachet,
there are flower projects to suit every mood.
Once you gain confidence and become inspired,
try experimenting with your own
designs and interpretations.

~Wild Garden~

Pictures such as "wild garden" opposite are closest to my heart. Born of a life-long obsession with flowers and gardening, they reflect my delightful garden. They are my flower borders, only better, because every plant is exactly where I want it to be with no bare soil and every nook and cranny occupied. The effect is rich and luxuriant but slightly mysterious, the composition suggesting hidden treasures.

These collages are therapeutic both to make and to examine. Your inspiration need not be restricted to the garden; remove the curtain of skeletonized leaves and colour-wash a blue sky and you can create a meadow picture. Hedgerow pictures are possible, even pictures inspired by fens and moors. Here, the backdrop of skeletonized leaves adds shadow, the mosses and lichens richness and texture, and the many and varied flowers, fascination. Keep the lower half of the picture dark and rich, then gradually introduce a variety of flowers, buds and leaves and allow them to fade away into an undulating horizon of spikes and blossoms.

ELEMENTS OF THE WILD GARDEN

Astrantia

Sea-holly

Fuchsia

Eryngium

Corkscrew rush

Blackberry

Pink cow parsley

Astilbe

Old rose

OTHER ELEMENTS

Baby's breath	Moss
Deutzia	Potentilla
Hydrangea	Sea carrot
Lichen	Skeletonized leaves

HOW TO MAKE A WILD GARDEN

1 Cut out a backing sheet to the required size and brush a thin layer of glue over it. Stick a patchwork of skeletonized leaves on to the backing, starting at the top and working gradually down towards the base.

2 Dip moss and lichens lightly in glue and then press them into place. Hold each flower spray with forceps and dab glue on the lower third of the stalk with an orange stick. Press the sprays in place.

3 Gradually fill in the collage. Hold each flower-head with forceps and dab a little glue in the centre. Stick them on the picture, small flowers in groups and larger blooms in an undulating horizon. Decorate the moss with small flower sprays.

4 Stick tiny flowers around the larger blooms. Add long spiky sprays by gluing and tucking the ends into the moss. Fill in any gaps between flowers with moss. Trim the bottom edge of the picture with scissors and glue it on to a mount.

The wild garden
*The rich green moss intensifies the deep reds and yellows
of the surrounding flowers, creating depth and mood.*

~ Plant Diary ~

Making a plant diary is a project that you can work on throughout the year. It will provide a visual record of your year, showing the changing seasons month by month, and reminding you, perhaps, of a sunny day in January, a summer holiday by the sea, visiting friends, or, perhaps, the lovely month of May.

January may not seem like the best time to start making a plant diary as winter gardens can be very bare. Yet there are early snowdrops, iris petals, scilla flowers, Christmas roses and lots of interesting leaves that can be collected and pressed. This early part of the year gives you plenty of time for planning your diary.

Choice of Flowers

With the advance of March and April, there will be a wider choice of flowers you can press, as daffodils, hellebores, primroses and marsh-marigolds will all be appearing. Lavish summer days will bring an abundance of colourful blossoms, such as roses, larkspurs and meadowsweet, to cram the pages of your plant diary. By September and October many flowers will be over, leaving you with the orange and brown autumn colours of burnet and ragwort, hips and berries.

You might like to label the flowers in your plant diary or, perhaps, add a word or two about where you collected them, or what the weather was like. This may give added interest when, at the end of the year, you leaf through your diary and look back on your year.

USEFUL EQUIPMENT

Saucer of rubber-based glue

Orange sticks

Scissors

Forceps

Very fine polyacetate-tipped pens

Flowers

February

February

A beautiful flower album
*This plant diary, open at January, provides a record of
the changing seasons of the year. The pages for
February (below left) and June (below) are ready to be inserted.*

~ *FlowerSampler* ~

Embroidered needlework samplers have an intrinsic beauty. Often worked on linen in a variety of stitches, patterns and techniques, they are always worthy of close scrutiny. The homespun charm of samplers seems to give a small glimpse into a past when time was not of the essence, and young girls (and occasionally boys) patiently and painstakingly stitched away.

A Formal Pattern

My flower samplers are based on traditional needlework samplers, and follow a formal and often symmetrical design. You can use linen or fine unbleached cotton as a mount and then build up the pattern with small flowers and leaves. Tiny rosebuds, florets of cow parsley, and dainty blooms of forget-me-not all look pretty on a flower sampler. Be wary about using very large blossoms and very loud and gaudy colours as they might be too dominant and detract from the overall design.

In this sampler I have made a border out of grains of rice placed end to end; the result looks very much like back-stitch and adds texture to the picture. The flowers and leaves used are all muted in colour and are reminiscent of old and faded embroidery threads. I have edged the sampler with hand-made lace and this adds to the feeling of an old textile.

The flowers and leaves could be arranged in an infinite variety of patterns. You could experiment using seeds, shells, beads and even ribbons with your flowers, and each sampler will have its individual charm.

Simple flower sampler
The subdued tones of pink, cream and green are set against the neutral linen background of the sampler to produce a warm and mellow effect.

ELEMENTS OF A FLOWER SAMPLER

Virginia creeper

Sea carrot

Pink cow parsley

Rice grains

Scabious

Hemlock
water-dropwort

Sycamore
seed capsules

Wood sage

Forget-me-not

Rosebuds

Astrantia

~ Summer Garlands ~

Whenever I think of garlands, I think first of Ophelia in Shakespeare's *Hamlet* with her fantastic garlands "of crow-flowers, nettles, daisies, and long purples". I think of decking and crowning with garlands, of "wreaths of the imagination", and all the garlands I have seen or read about, in embroidery and painting, in folklore, on porcelain and on decorative furniture. Inspiration for pressed flower garlands is everywhere. They can be simple or rich, romantically entwined with ribbons or embellished with streamers. They can even be glittering theatrical affairs on frosted backgrounds.

Flower Combinations

All pressed flowers are appropriate for garlands. Use leaves and mosses to give depth, and spindly grasses, buds and sprays to edge your garlands. Try unusual combinations: lovage and great wood-rush for lacy edges, the tiny florets of cow parsley on moss, the lovely green umbels of hemlock water-dropwort mixed with the bright orange and yellow potentilla flowers. Tiny, plump pearl everlasting buds look wonderful dotted amongst moss and lichen. You might scatter the flowers, buds and leaves from the pretty threepenny-bit rose through your scheme, or make tiny circlets of flowers to adorn special cards. Put romance into your garlands by twisting fragile ribbons through your flowers and adding thin bows of silk.

Little garland card
A circlet of moss surrounded by delicate midsummer blooms.

ELEMENTS OF THE SUMMER GARLAND

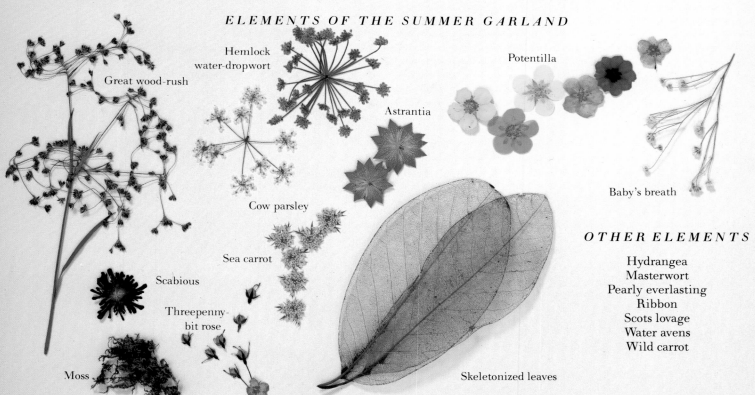

Great wood-rush

Hemlock water-dropwort

Potentilla

Astrantia

Cow parsley

Baby's breath

Sea carrot

Scabious

Threepenny-bit rose

Moss

Skeletonized leaves

OTHER ELEMENTS

Hydrangea
Masterwort
Pearly everlasting
Ribbon
Scots lovage
Water avens
Wild carrot

A touch of romance
The bright flowers of the garland are softened
with frills of cow parsley
and a wispy trail of great wood-rush.

Wedding Bouquet

When you catch the bride's bouquet at a wedding, what do you do with it? Do you wrap it in tissue paper and let it gather dust in a trunk in the attic? A much more romantic idea is to turn it into a wedding bouquet picture, the perfect memento of a happy day.

The picture opposite was made with the flowers from a very lavish wedding bouquet; there were enough flowers to make a border in addition to the central arrangement. I wanted to create a picture that was romantic and pretty, to reflect the atmosphere of a wedding. So I used a pale pink colour wash for the background and added a border of antique lace. You could use the lace from the bride's gown, or even mount the entire picture on the fabric of the bride's dress. For interest I added a few extra seasonal flowers in keeping with the theme of the picture: tiny forget-me-nots and violets gathered from my garden, and florets of lovely lime-yellow alexanders that were blooming at the time in our hedgerows.

Pressing a Bouquet

When you come to pressing a wedding bouquet, the flowers will not be very fresh and may need reviving. So dismantle the bouquet and then pop the flowers in a polythene bag. Put this in the fridge for an hour or so, before you begin pressing. You should start pressing the flowers as soon as possible to retain their lovely colours.

I find that there is always an element of surprise involved when pressing flowers for the first time. When I was making this wedding bouquet picture I was amazed and delighted with the final colours. So cross your fingers and have a go too!

**ELEMENTS OF
THE WEDDING BOUQUET**

Roses

Hellebore

Baby's-breath

Cherry blossom

Alexanders

Larkspur

Variegated ivy

Forget-me-not

OTHER ELEMENTS

Allium
Common dog-violet
Heather
Hyacinth
Lace
Statice

Fern

A romantic memento
These exquisite pressed flowers from
a wedding bouquet are set against a pale
pink background and surrounded
with fine lace.

· 77 ·

Flower Baskets

What about creating a moss-lined "basket" using bracken fronds and making it overflow with pressed flowers, mosses, lichens and skeletonized leaves? You can mingle and use plant material gathered during all four seasons, including thin flower spikes of plantain and dock, panicles of wild clematis and ragwort, marigolds, buttercups, astrantias and avens, in fact any plant material from the cornucopia available to us.

Inspirational Ideas

The picture opposite has a strong orange bias, but most combinations will look lovely and give a feeling of rural abundance. A bowl of June flowers, a rich canvas of blossoms and fruits, a collection of blooms from your own garden — all these could be inspirational when filling your basket. Try mixing the unlikely — an unfurling fern frond and a new green seedhead for example, or oats with wild clematis. Avoid adding material that looks clumsy, however. If a stalk is too thick, then pare it to a sliver, and if necessary fillet fern fronds so that the eye is drawn to the intriguing ammonite curl and not to a thick, fuzzy stalk! It is best to begin with an outline of bold, spiky plants and then fill the gaps with smaller flowers.

You can spray the bracken basket a different colour and embellish it with lichens, overflowing blossoms, or even a snail shell. Quaint old wicker baskets are a good source of inspiration. Stand well back from your picture and assess the balance, remembering that the material used should appear to sit in the basket comfortably. If there is a jarring note then stick something over it — rich green moss can work miracles when all else fails.

ELEMENTS OF THE FLOWER BASKET

Astrantia

Meadow oat-grass

Potentilla

Ragwort

Clematis

Montbretia

Young fern frond

Hydrangea

OTHER ELEMENTS

Bracken	Goldenrod	Primula
Burnet	Lady's-mantle	Sea-holly
Everlasting	Lichen	Skeletonized leaves
Ferns	Moss	Wild carrot

HOW TO MAKE A FLOWER BASKET

1 Cut out a basket shape from a piece of card. Dip moss lightly in a saucer of glue and then stick it on the basket shape. Pack the clumps of moss tightly, making sure that no card is visible.

2 Trim several bracken fronds to the size of the basket. Dab glue along each frond with an orange stick, then, using forceps, stick the fronds on the moss. Select the flowers to be displayed.

3 Glue the basket on to a mount. Arrange bold and spiky plant material in a skeleton outline above the basket and glue in place. Fill in with groups of blossoms, long-stemmed fern fronds, moss and lichens.

High summer basket
Both the colour scheme of bold oranges, with yellows, browns and greens, and the overflowing
composition of this picture suggest the abundance of midsummer.

~ Greetings Cards ~

Greetings cards are easy and rewarding to make and there are many decorative styles that you can use.

A "Get Well" card, decorated with a posy of pretty and varied flowers, will constantly draw the eyes of someone confined to bed. A garland of blossoms surrounding an inscription could be made into a birthday or anniversary card. Festive Christmas cards provide the ideal opportunity to experiment with gold and silver paint and glitter, as well as with seasonal plants and berries. Time and thought should be spent creating a truly romantic Valentine card; choose the prettiest lace and the loveliest silk, and take time to select your most beautiful flowers. A hand-made card can often mean far more to the recipient than one that has been bought.

Bookmarks and Gift Tags

These can be decorated in a similar way to the greetings cards, using a variety of styles, but on a smaller scale. Little gift labels decorated with the tips of flower spikes, newly formed leaves, tiny florets and small unopened buds can all look enchanting.

The arrangement of the flowers on bookmarks should be slightly elongated to keep a sense of balance on the long narrow piece of card. To complete the bookmark or gift tag, punch a hole at the bottom of the card, and then loop through a length of ribbon.

MAKING A CARD

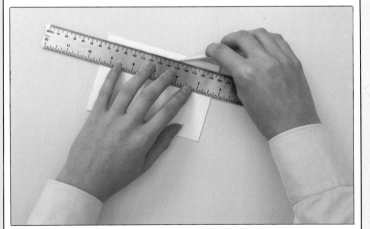

Cut out a rectangle of hand-made paper to measure approximately 18 cm long by 12 cm wide (8 x 4 in). Fold the paper in half lengthways. Place a ruler about 2 mm (⅛ in) from the edge of the fold as shown above and hold it firmly in place with one hand. Holding a bone folder (or an appropriate substitute) in your other hand, run it over the paper along the edge of the ruler, to flatten and sharpen the fold. You can now decorate the front of your card with pressed flowers and leaves.

Bookmarks and gift tags (above)
These decorative bookmarks and gift tags were very easy to make. The simplest design consists of a single specimen flower framed in a narrow border, while the more abstract design is a "random" collage of flowers and leaves, cut into rectangular shapes, and then glued on the bookmark or tag.

Random flower collage (below)
*A colourful, abstract
design of blossoms,
leaves and mosses.*

Festive Christmas wreath (above)
*This tiny wreath was made with ivy
leaves, berries and fir leaves and
decorated with a bright red ribbon.*

Romantic Valentine card (above)
*A heart made from threepenny-bit
rosebuds and frilled lace is framed by
a pretty lace border.*

Garland card (above)
*A simple yet effective
design of tiny forget-
me-nots, violets, ivy
leaves and avens.*

A seashore theme (above)
*A pleasing arrangement of seaside
plants, shells and seaweeds make for
an unusual greetings card.*

Favourite summer flowers (above)
*A bouquet arrangement of small summer
flowers is displayed simply against a
contrasting background.*

~Kitchen Posters~

There's no need to limit your pressing just to flowers and leaves. Why not experiment with fruit and vegetables? When pressed, fruit and vegetables retain their bright and cheerful colours and interesting textures and shapes. There is plenty of scope for experimentation and you can try making both formal and abstract, free-style pictures.

These kitchen posters were made entirely from a mixture of traditional and exotic fruit and vegetables which I bought from my local greengrocers, and I had great fun making them. The dominant colours are orange and red, in the form of sliced carrots, kumquats, chilli peppers and tiny red lentils. These colours contrast well with the dark green strawberry leaves, parsley sprigs, French beans and split peas. The varied and unusual textures such as feathery alfalfa sprouts and knobbly peas and beans give added interest.

You could try pressing cross-sections of other fruit and vegetables, such as cucumber and baby sweetcorn, or whole bunches of tiny grapes. You can also combine pressed fruit with flowers to create a "wild fruit garden" or "orchard collage". Just experiment and have fun!

ELEMENTS OF A KITCHEN POSTER

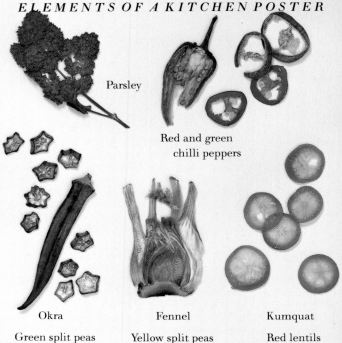

Parsley

Red and green
chilli peppers

Okra

Fennel

Kumquat

Green split peas   Yellow split peas   Red lentils

OTHER ELEMENTS

Alfalfa sprouts	Mange tout
Carrots	Mushrooms
Fennel	Red cabbage
French beans	Rhubarb
Kiwi fruit	Strawberries

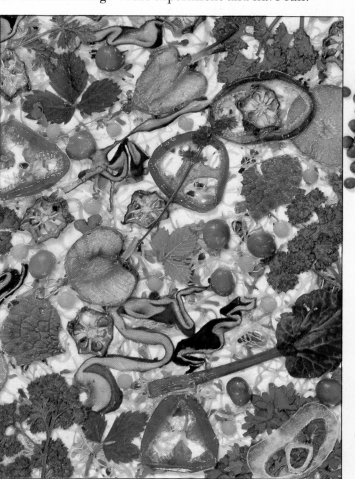

Vegetable garden (left)
This abstract design of bright orange carrots, red chilli peppers, and fresh green peas and parsley leaves looks very effective against the pale yellow background.

Edible decoration (right)
Specimens of fruit and vegetables are framed in an oval of alfalfa sprouts and parsley, and surrounded by a formal arrangement of lentils and vegetables.

Summer Frieze

My summer frieze is a rich repetitive pattern of colourful midsummer flowers, moss and lichens, set against a Mediterranean blue sky. The undulating horizon of pastel potentilla blossoms is punctuated by the dark crimson blooms of the large old rose, the dominant feature of the frieze. The upright forms of larkspur and meadow oat-grass balance the collage and emphasize the repetitive design.

You don't need a wide variety of flowers and leaves to create a frieze; a simple narrow border can be just as effective as my detailed summer frieze. An important part of the design, however, is one dominant colour occurring at regular intervals which will immediately draw your eye to the repeating pattern. You can use any intensely coloured flower, leaf or seedhead and then surround it with paler blooms for a pretty, faded contrast.

Friezes can look delightful hung over a bed or above a mantelpiece, or used as an interesting border around a room, or pressed flower picture.

ELEMENTS OF A SUMMER FRIEZE

Sea carrot

Guelder-rose

Speedwell

Lady's-mantle

Old rose

Potentilla

Larkspur

Hydrangea

Baby's
breath

Hemlock
water-dropwort

Meadow oat-grass

Lichen

Scabious

Astrantia

Fuchsia

Moss

Skeletonized leaf

Colourful summer flowers
The contrasting colours, textures and shapes
of the different blossoms, spikes, mosses and lichens
combine to create a dramatic and luxuriant summer frieze.

~ Seasonal Series ~

In this series of four oval pictures I have tried to evoke the atmosphere of the four seasons, using flowers and leaves found growing in each season. To enhance the theme I have colour-washed the background of spring in a fresh pale green, summer in sky blue and autumn in burnt orange; winter I have left white.

The Four Seasons

Spring is the time when buds burst into glorious flower and new shoots and leaves begin to sprout. My spring picture conveys this feeling of freshness with bright yellow buttercups and daffodils and the lovely flowering cherry. Unfurling fern fronds and newly opened hazel catkins add further spring interest.

A summer collage is very easy to make as there is such a wide choice of flowers available. I have used old roses, potentillas, avens and astrantia in the centre of the collage, and nursery pink and blue larkspurs to give height and balance.

Autumn is the season of "mellow fruitfulness", when rich golden browns, oranges and yellows predominate. In my autumn collage I have mingled bright potentilla blossoms with an array of seedheads and the rich brown shuttlecock fern.

If you really search the woods, hedgerows and your garden during the winter you will find a surprising amount of plant material. In my winter picture snowdrops nestle amongst the moss and lichen at the base of the oval while alder catkins and pussy willow strengthen the top. Welcome colour is provided by lovely 'de Caen' anemone blossoms, which you can buy and then press, and variegated ivy.

Spring
Two purple hellebores add interest to the greens and yellows of spring.

Summer
This summer collage overflows with an abundance of colourful blooms.

ELEMENTS OF A SEASONAL SERIES

Spring	*Summer*	*Autumn*	*Winter*
Bridewort	Astrantia	Astrantia	Alder catkins
Buttercup	Avens	Bellflower	Anemone
Corkscrew rush	Cow parsley	Blackberry	Hogweed
Daffodil	Hemlock water-dropwort	Burnet	Ivy
Flowering cherry	Lady's-mantle	Coreopsis	Lichen
Guelder-rose	Larkspur	Dock	Moss
Hart's-tongue fern	Lesser quaking-grass	Hogweed	Snowdrop
Hazel catkins	Lichen	Honesty	Skeletonized leaves
Hellebore	Meadowsweet	Hop	Toadstool
Lichen	Meadow oat-grass	Ivy	Witch hazel
Maidenhair fern	Moss	Meadowsweet	Wood woundwort
Marsh-marigold	Old rose	Potentilla	
Moss	Potentilla	Ragwort	
Pink cow parsley	Sea carrot	Rose hips	
Polyanthus	Skeletonized leaves	Shuttlecock fern	
Primrose		Skeletonized leaves	
Ragged-robin			
Skeletonized leaves			

Autumn

Rich brown leaves and seedheads are brightened by orange autumn flowers.

Winter

Bright red anemones add a festive touch to this crisp winter collage.

~ *Perfumed Sachets* ~

These pretty sachets, gently perfumed with pot pourri, can be made in a wide variety of different shapes, sizes and materials. Cotton, linen, calico, lace, muslin or silk are all suitable fabrics. Edges can be pinked or trimmed with lace; pretty ribbons can be stitched or glued on and any small pressed flowers can be used to decorate your sachets: a tiny spray or posy of flowers, a garland, or just a single specimen will all look charming.

Pot Pourri Filling

Pot pourri can be bought ready mixed, or can be made from flowers and leaves gathered in your garden which are then mixed with flower essences and fixatives (see page 106). The bought varieties are available in such evocative mixtures as "Cottage Garden", "Rose Garden", and rose petal and lavender. A good idea is to match the pot pourri filling with the pressed flower decoration. For example, you could fill a rose-decorated sachet with "Rose Garden" pot pourri, or decorate a sachet of dried balm, mint and bergamot with a few sprigs of pressed herbs, or use a mixture of peppermint leaves and flowers. In fact, there are endless combinations to be tried.

These sweetly scented sachets can be used everywhere. Place them in drawers or in a linen cupboard where they will gently perfume the contents; tuck them inside your pillow case for a soothing scent at night, or loop the little gathered bags of pot pourri over radiators where the warmth will encourage the flower oils to evaporate and perfume the room. Lace sachets also look pretty displayed on dressing tables and bedside tables, or in the bathroom propped on a shelf.

Simple lace bag (above left)
and flat lace calico sachets (above)

HOW TO MAKE A PERFUMED SACHET

1 Cut out two squares of fabric with pinking shears. On one piece draw the stitching guide in pencil. Lightly glue the flowers and leaves and position them on the fabric. Name them neatly with a fine indelible pen.

2 Pin the two pieces of fabric together. Using a zig-zag stitch, sew a strip of lace around three sides of the sachet, through the two layers of fabric. Start at the base of the fabric and follow the stitching guide round. Remove the pins.

3 Fill the sachet with pot pourri. Using a zig-zag stitch complete the sewing on of the lace to close the sachet. Join and mitre the lace at the bottom right-hand corner, using a plain stitch. Trim the lace and iron it lightly.

Coloured silk taffeta sachets

Frilled lace calico sachets *(right)*

ELEMENTS OF A PERFUMED SACHET

Ribbon

Needles and thimble

Pot pourri

Fabric

Cotton thread

Lace

Cottage Garden Herbal

This picture is a simple botanical arrangement of plants, reminiscent of a page from an ancient herbal. These plants all used to be grown in traditional cottage gardens, and they have all played a part in herbal lore: some were used as medicinal herbs, others were used as sweet-smelling additions to pot pourri, washballs, pomanders, and other aromatic articles of the past, while others were — and still are — used in cooking.

Of course there are many other plants that are suitable for this kind of "herbal" picture — you need not keep "cottage garden" as your theme. You could choose plants for their association with the past, some for their shape and colour, and others, perhaps, for their scent. This is a picture where you can apply your own individual interpretation.

Building up the Picture

It takes time and a good deal of care to make a well balanced picture. You should arrange the specimen plants in such a way that no bloom is dominant, and then fill in the gaps with long, thin plants. Make sure you leave enough white background for each specimen plant to be clearly seen and labelled.

The arched flower border is made with small flowerbuds, petals and leaves, haphazardly crammed together. Florets of sea carrot and cow parsley can be scattered along the border to fill in any odd gaps. You can make a slightly more formal arrangement at the apex of the arch, as in the cottage garden herbal, but it should blend discreetly with the rest of the border.

Part of the general appeal of the picture is that the plants are named so you know what you are looking at. I use the plants' common everyday names, rather than the Latin, as some of them are so fascinating — you *have* to take a second look at plants with names like woad, hemlock and Good-King-Henry!

ELEMENTS OF A COTTAGE GARDEN HERBAL

Astrantia	Mint
Borage	Moss
Chamomile	'Mundi' rose
Fennel	Nipplewort
Feverfew	Oak fern
Ginger mint	Old rose
Good-King-Henry	Pink cow parsley
Hemlock water-dropwort	Sage
Lichen	Sea carrot
Lovage	Threepenny-bit rose
Maidenhair spleenwort	Vervain
Meadowsweet	Woad

An old-fashioned display
Specimen plants are singled out
for attention while a colourful assortment
of blooms provides a decorative border.

Fern

Fennel

Scented Old
Rose

Nipplewort

Borage

Woad

Green
Sage

Purple Sage

Meadowsweet

Mint

Mundi Rose

Lichen

Vervain

Fern

Chamomile

Threepenny-Bit
Rose

Good-King-
Henry

AGRIMONY ANGELICA ALECOST ANISE ARNICA BORAGE BALM

DEADNETTLE CHICORY WOAD HEMLOCK WORMWOOD CHERVIL CHICORY

Cottage Garden Herbs

Penny Black
August '86

～ Lace Pillows ～

I have always been fascinated by beautiful antique textiles and love to explore the tiny tucks sewn with old-fashioned steel needles, the intricate whitework embroidery on muslin, and those exquisite Honiton, Hamilton and Limerick laces. Old lace has such intrinsic charm that even the smallest scraps, appliquéd on to calico, will look pretty.

Making the Pillow

My scented lace pillows are really an extension of these interests and are quite easy to make. You will need two square or rectangular pieces of calico, of equal size, some oddments of lace, and pressed flowers to decorate the front. Around one piece of calico pencil a border marginally wider than the lace that will frill your pillow. Back this piece of calico with lightweight synthetic wadding and tack it into place. Arrange your lace within the pencilled rectangle or square, pin it into place and hand-sew along every edge, making sure that your stitches go through the lace, calico and synthetic wadding. This produces a soft quilted effect. Next, hand-sew your frill of lace around the outside edges of your appliquéd lace. With right sides together, stitch the two pieces of calico together along three sides and turn them the right side out. Stuff the pillow with synthetic wadding that has been filled with pot pourri and sew up the last edge. Decorate the pillow with pressed flowers, gluing them into place. Sew a piece of bridal veiling over the front of your pillow, to protect the flower decoration.

A few lace pillows scattered around the bedroom or arranged on the bed can look very charming. Or you could prop a few cushions on your settee or favourite armchair. In fact, lace pillows will add a touch of romance and nostalgia wherever they are used.

A striped effect (right)
This simple cushion is covered with stripes of white, cream and coffee-coloured lace to enhance the posy of roses.

A formal decoration
(far right)
A garland of roses, cow parsley and sea carrot decorates the front of this elegant lace pillow.

~Decorated Furniture~

Decorating furniture with pressed flowers and leaves is a very old art. With its lovely rural charm it is reminiscent of cottage parlours, Provencale kitchens and old canal barges. Mellow stripped pine is an ideal surface to decorate, and decorated tin can also look pretty. You can give a new lease of life to chests-of-drawers, cupboard doors, jewellery boxes, and even kitchen chairs, by decorating them with posies, borders, swags or garlands of pressed flowers and leaves. Even fern fronds, simply arranged, look charming.

It is best to use flat flowers and leaves as you have to apply several coats of varnish to the article of furniture after it has been decorated, and textured material would be too bulky and impractical. Small ornate leaves and blossoms are best and fit easily into a design; gilded leaves can also be used and look stunning when applied to black lacquered boxes. If you can, avoid flowers that are likely to become transparent when varnished, such as hydrangea and potentilla blossoms; it is best to experiment with your flowers before using them.

Candles

Pressed flowers can look beautiful when they are applied to candles. When the candles are lit, the flowers become translucent, and look very pretty. Use small, delicate specimens rather than large fussy arrangements of flowers for a more simple charm. Try to arrange your flowers near the base of the candle except, perhaps, for the odd little forget-me-not, or long fern tendril, or they may catch fire in the candle flame.

I like to use hand-made candles which are often available in florists or craft shops, though ordinary kitchen candles can look equally charming. White candles are preferable as nothing then distracts from the beauty and colour of the flowers.

To decorate the candle, hold the flower in place on the candle and then brush a thin film of melted wax over it. For a smoother result you can dip the candle into a pan of melted wax, but this can be dangerous for the novice and I advise extreme caution.

Decorative candles
Delicate trailing fern fronds and tiny fragile blossoms provide a simple decoration for plain white candles.

Candle box
A charming arrangement of snowdrops and ivy leaves transforms an old pine candle box that had previously been banished to the attic.

Ornamental mirror frame

This pine mirror frame is prettily decorated with simple corner arrangements of roses, potentilla, astrantia and hydrangea blossoms for a cottage-like effect.

Photograph Frames

Pressed flowers and leaves can look lovely decorating a photograph frame. Simple card frames can be transformed with anything from a few forget-me-nots displayed in a corner to a colourful tapestry of anemones and hellebores.

You can create a formal stylized pattern using just a few select flowers, perhaps of the same colour or size; or for a more romantic feel twist thin lengths of ribbon through your flowers and edge the corners of the frame with lace. You could even add beads and shells or a sprinkling of glitter for a more theatrical effect. Make sure that the plant material you use is smooth and flat; bulky textures can look too heavy and overpowering.

Simple elegance (below)
*Large pink and purple blossoms decorate
the foot of this frame while dainty ivy leaves
seem to climb up its sides.*

***Tapestry of
flowers*** (right)
*Bright summer
flowers jostle for
space in this
colourful random
design.*

Summer colours (above)
*Trailing ferns hang down
from an arrangement of
pretty summer blooms.*

Further Techniques

*This section details the practical
aspects of making pressed flower collages,
including a guide to the different presses available,
advice on when to gather flowers,
and how to press them quickly so that their
colours are retained. There is also a garden plan
that includes some of the best plants
to grow for pressing, as well as a look at
the associated skills of making pot pourri,
fabric dyeing and picture framing.*

~*Flower Presses*~

If you have never pressed any flowers before, you may feel a little unsure as to which press to start off with. It certainly need not be anything too elaborate: for a couple of years I used only a makeshift press, consisting of two pieces of plywood and three bricks! From this, I progressed on to a good homemade working press, and it has only been in the last year that I have had my professional, heavy-duty press. Of course, this is the best type of press to use, but it is not necessary in the beginning.

Choosing a Press

It is possible to press flowers in a magazine or book as a temporary measure. To apply pressure, put a heavy weight on top, or else insert the magazine or book under the carpet in a spot where there is a lot of coming and going, or under the cushion of a well-used chair: necessity must be the mother of invention! However, I would only recommend this in an emergency, when you have nothing else you can use. A makeshift press is a good press to start off with. It is very cheap to make; all you need are two spare pieces of plywood and some heavy weights such as bricks. Place your material to be pressed in between tissues or one-way nappy liners and place these between sheets of absorbent paper (the illustration opposite shows

a breakdown of the layers of paper to use). Then sandwich all these layers between your pieces of plywood and place three bricks or similar heavy weights on top. This type of press has the advantage of maintaining constant pressure whilst the flowers and leaves dry out. Other presses have to be tightened continually.

If you are prepared to spend some money on a more advanced press, you should consider progressing on to a simple, traditional press. You can either buy one or make one. A traditional press usually works by tightening four wing nuts and bolts, one at each corner of the press, which slowly presses the plant material that is sandwiched in layers of paper in the middle.

Then, if you find you want a stronger press, you can't do better than a heavy-duty professional press. You can press absolutely anything in one of these presses, including very bulky and textured plant material, which of course gives you a greater variety of material to work with. The professional press works by a central screw, and is less bothersome to use than four wing nuts and bolts (see page 120 for addresses of suppliers).

Always make sure that your presses are stored in a dry place with a good circulation of air, to guard against damp and mildew, the arch enemies of pressed flowers.

Makeshift press

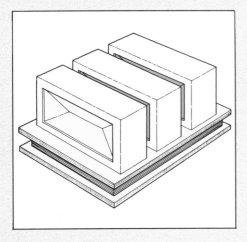

This is an excellent press for a beginner. You need two pieces of plywood and three bricks. Place your flowers between layers of absorbent paper (see the illustration opposite) and sandwich these between the pieces of plywood. Then place the bricks on top.

Travelling press

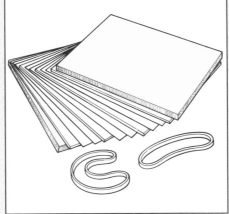

This is ideal for carrying with you when you are gathering flowers. It consists of two small pieces of plywood between which you sandwich the flowers in layers of absorbent paper (see the illustration opposite). The press is held together by two elastic bands.

Emergency press

In an emergency you can press flowers between the pages of a book or magazine. Turn over the first six pages and insert a layer of tissues, then the flowers, and then another layer of tissues. Gently close the book and place a heavy weight on top.

Layers in a press

Plywood board

Wing nut

Three sheets of
folded recycled paper

Two layers of tissues
or one-way nappy liners

Three sheets of
folded recycled paper

Bolt

Plywood board

TRADITIONAL PRESS

A traditional flower press can be bought from most craft shops or, alternatively, you can make one yourself. It consists of two pieces of heavy-gauge plywood, which form the top and bottom of the press, and these are joined at the corners by four wing nuts and bolts. There is space in the press for up to twenty or thirty layers of absorbent paper and I use the following order for the layers: three sheets of folded recycled paper, one layer of tissues or one-way nappy liners on which you put your flowers, followed by another layer of tissues or one-way nappy liners and three more sheets of folded recycled paper.

Assembled press

~Gathering & Preparation~

When gathering plant material for pressing, take only as much as you need. Try to leave behind plenty of buds and flowers, especially when gathering from the wild. In fact it is against the law to pick or uproot any rare wild plant (see page 116 for a list of protected plants). You can try gathering a little of everything to begin with — single blossoms, sprays, leaves, buds, seedheads, and even the occasional plant complete with roots. Try the unexpected: stinging nettles, iris and lily petals, trailing wands of climbing plants, and bunches of newly formed grapes.

Flowers should be at their best when you pick them, when their colours are richest. This is usually when they have just opened, not when they have been flowering for some time. The petals should be clean, undamaged and fresh. It is important to gather your plant material on a dry day as dampness encourages mildew; the afternoon is best as any morning dew will have evaporated by then. In an absolute emergency, however, wet flowers can be picked and left to dry in a vase of water indoors.

When you are collecting plant material, put the specimens in a polythene bag to keep them fresh. Don't overfill the bag, though, in case the flowers crush each other. Before you seal the bag, blow air into it and then secure the open end with a plastic tie. This air pocket prevents the flowers from becoming crushed, dried out or too hot. If the flowers have wilted by the time you get home, put the polythene bag with its contents in the fridge or a cool place until they perk up again.

Plant material should be pressed as soon as possible after it has been picked, to retain its colour, but some preparation will be required first. When handling single blossoms and delicate buds, use forceps or tweezers to avoid damaging the petals.

Preparing Different Blossoms

Single blossoms, such as potentilla and meadow buttercup, press flat very easily, with or without their stalks. Cut the stalks off with sharp scissors if you do not want them. Sprays of flowers, such as hydrangea or forget-me-not, can be pressed whole or separated into individual blooms. Use sharp scissors to cut off each bloom, being very careful not to damage the petals.

Some double flowers benefit from being thinned out. Cut the flower-head off the stalk, then carefully pluck out a few of the central petals, to make a flatter flower-head. Three-dimensional flowers, such as rosebuds and daffodils,

Slicing flower-heads

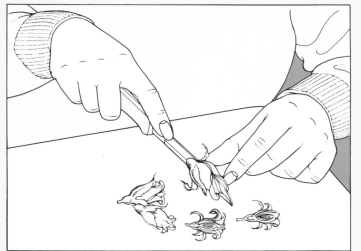

Slice bulky, three-dimensional flower-heads, such as rosebuds and daffodils, in half lengthways before pressing them. To do this, hold the flower-head steady on a table and carefully cut through it, from the tip to the base, with a sharp knife. Both halves of the flower-head can then be used, and since each half has a flat surface, this makes it easier to glue them on to the flower picture.

Preparing vegetables

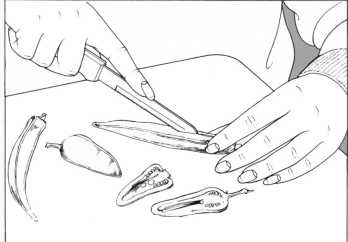

Slice long, thin vegetables, such as okra and chilli peppers, either lengthways or widthways before pressing them. To do this, hold the vegetable steady on a table, between finger and thumb, and then slice through it with a sharp knife, drawing the knife away from your hand. Remove any stray seeds or strands of vegetable skin, and blot any juicy or wet areas with a tissue.

can be cut in half lengthways with scissors or a scalpel, before being pressed. You can then use both halves in your picture. Alternatively, you can press the flower whole for a more textured effect. You will need to make a "collar" (see the illustration) for flowers that have thick centres, to keep the petals pressed flat, without unduly squashing the flower centre, when pressing the flower.

Unusual Plant Material

If you are unable to obtain some flowers, you can always use *dried flowers*. Before pressing them, hold them in the steam from a kettle to revitalize them.

Most *lichens, mosses* and *barks* need not be pressed. I arrange them on a tray and leave them in a warm, dry spot for a day or so, by which time they will be ready for use. If the material is not flat enough for use then a few hours in a press will flatten them, but I think that half the beauty of this plant material is its texture.

Tiny *toadstools* do not need any preparation before pressing, but larger *fungi* can be cut in half lengthways, or into cross-sections, before being pressed lightly. I only press material that I can positively identify as being non-poisonous. Before pressing segments of *seaweed*, wash them thoroughly in tap water to remove the salty sea water and then dab them dry with tissues.

Fruit and *vegetables*, such as beans, chillies, okra, peppers and most soft fruit, can be cut in half lengthways, or into cross-sections, before being pressed. You can remove the fruit skin or rind and press this separately.

Steaming dried flowers

Hold dried flowers in the steam from a boiling kettle for a minute or so before pressing them. The moist steam will revitalize the flowers. Be careful not to scald yourself; it is best to steam only long-stemmed flowers, so that your hands are kept out of the steam.

Making a collar

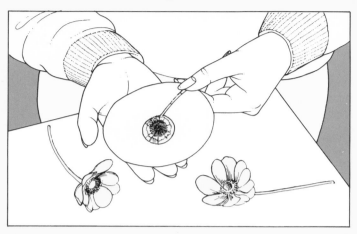

To make a flower collar, cut out a piece of blotting paper the size of the flower-head. Cut a hole in the middle of this the same size as the bulky centre. Place this collar over the flower so the flower centre protrudes through the hole. Add further collars until the top of the flower centre is level with the top layer of collars.

Thinning sprays of flowers

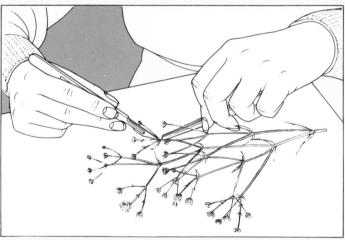

Sprays of flowers, such as lady's-mantle and baby's breath may require thinning before they are pressed. Using tweezers or forceps to avoid crushing the flowers, hold the spray steady on a flat surface. With a scalpel carefully slice off smaller stalks throughout the spray where necessary. You can use scissors instead of a scalpel if you prefer, though the results may not be as neat.

~ *Pressing & Storage* ~

Whatever type of press you use the basic and essential rules of pressing are the same. Speed is of the essence when pressing plant material, and the quicker your material is dried, the brighter the colours will remain.

First you have to build up layers of absorbent paper in the press. I use folded sheets of recycled paper and then a layer of one-way nappy liners, plus extra tissues for juicy plant material, but you can use blotting paper, sugar paper, or newspaper. Lay your flowers and leaves carefully on the nappy liners or tissues, putting as many as possible on to the sheet without them overlapping. Keep material of a similar thickness on the same sheet as this will ensure that the entire sheet receives uniform pressure. Also try to keep *similar* flowers and leaves together as this makes life easier when you are working on your collages.

Cover the material with another layer of nappy liners or tissues and more layers of recycled paper, making sure that the flowers and leaves are not dislodged in the process. These layers should be repeated for each batch of specimens. To apply the correct pressure, tighten the screws on the press until they become stiff.

Unusual Plant Material

When pressing succulent plant material, such as *fruit and vegetables, toadstools* and *fungi*, use very gentle pressure and change the paper and tissues frequently. *Dried flowers*, on the other hand, require very strong pressure.

Quick Drying

I try to dry everything in about two weeks or less (with the exception of fruit and vegetables), by regularly changing the damp recycled paper with dry paper. For the first three or four days, you should change or dry the paper at least once a day. After that you can leave it for two or more days, depending on how dry your material actually is. But remember, *do not* take your specimens out of the

BUILDING THE LAYERS IN A PRESS

1 Fold three sheets of recycled paper in half lengthways and place these in the press. Lay a fourth sheet of recycled paper, folded, on top of these and then open it out again, so that one half of the paper is outside the edge of the press.

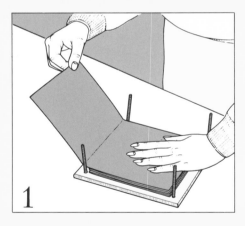

2 Place a layer of one-way nappy liners on top of the recycled paper layers. If you are pressing succulent plant material, such as fruit and vegetables, place an extra layer of tissues in between the recycled paper and the nappy liners.

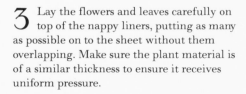

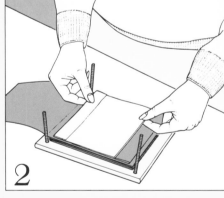

3 Lay the flowers and leaves carefully on top of the nappy liners, putting as many as possible on to the sheet without them overlapping. Make sure the plant material is of a similar thickness to ensure it receives uniform pressure.

4 Cover the plant material with another layer of nappy liners (and an extra layer of tissues if pressing succulent plant material) and then refold the last sheet of recycled paper over the top. Place a further three sheets on top to complete the layers.

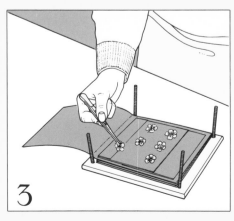

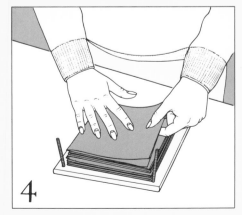

actual nappy liners or tissues on which they have been arranged, as they will be very frail and easily damaged.

Dry the paper in a warm place, such as over a radiator or chair in a warm dry room, or in an airing cupboard. I often return warm paper to the press as this speeds up the drying process. But make sure the paper is not *too* hot or you may end up with "casseroled" flowers! Test the plant material for dryness: if the flowers feel cold and clammy, they are not ready; when they feel crisp and warm, they are dry and ready to use.

Dry Storage

Store the material in a dry place to guard against mould, the arch enemy of pressed flower material. It is advisable to put a sheet of corrugated paper between every dozen or so layers of specimens as this will help the air to circulate. I keep my material in a random fashion, so there is an element of surprise when looking through the sheets, which can result in an inspired collage.

Pressed plant material is prone to attack by small mites that will eventually reduce it to dust. Keep a constant check and at the first sign of these microscopic creatures, give them a quick puff of animal flea powder; this will banish them forever.

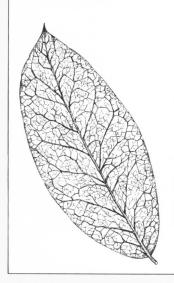

Skeletonized leaves
If you can't find any skeletonized leaves, it is easy to make your own. Collect a supply of leaves in mid-summer (magnolia leaves are the best) and soak them in rainwater for a month to soften the leaf tissue. Then rinse the leaves under running water, and brush them gently with a soft brush to remove the softened tissue. Allow the leaves to dry and then iron them carefully.

STORING PRESSED FLOWERS

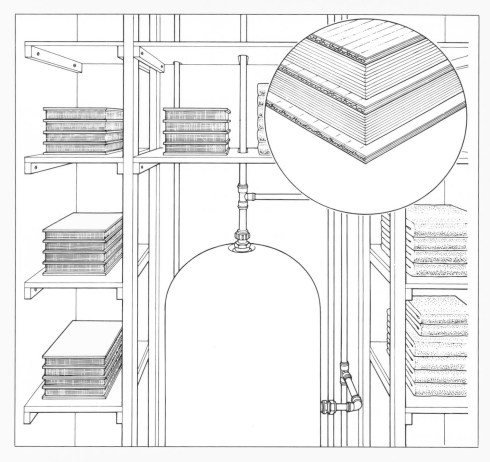

Using your linen cupboard
Store your pressed flowers and other plant material in a dry place with a good circulation of air, to guard against damp and mould. A linen or airing cupboard is ideal, if you have the room. Keep the pressed plant material in the sheet of recycled paper in which it was pressed, but remove the top layer of nappy liners. Stack the sheets one on top of the other, with a sheet of corrugated paper between every dozen of so layers of specimens, to help the air circulate.

~Tricks of the Trade~

When you first start making your flower collages you will probably feel a little nervous at the prospect of handling fragile blossoms and you are bound to make mistakes and damage the odd flower, or break a stalk or two. Don't worry about this: with practice you will find ways and means of transforming, substituting, altering, improving and mending your work. Damaged material can easily be mended by patching, by hiding the offending portion with something else, or simply by removing and replacing the damaged material. Rubber-based glue is ideal for those who are constantly changing their minds or making mistakes.

Plant material can be joined and altered in a host of ways. If the angle of a stalk or spray offends, then you can carefully break portions off and re-align them when gluing them on to your picture. If you encounter a problem there is almost certainly a way round it, even if you are reduced to cutting up a precious picture and making it into cards! I once ran out of glue when experimenting with a collage but successfully completed it using marmalade!

You can also indulge in a little pressed flower *trompe-l'oeil*. The shapes of leaves can be changed; you can construct your own "designer-made" flowers from odd left-over petals, flower centres, leaves and stalks; or you can make large and complicated flowers out of a graded series of smaller ones placed one on top of the other. Of course as you become more experienced, you will learn to cut corners as well. Pressed flowers is a time-consuming craft and any short cut is worth remembering. Listed below are some of the "tricks of the trade" I have discovered over the years.

CUTTING CORNERS

Spraying seedheads

Dried seedheads can look very pretty in a flower picture. However, the seeds are liable to fall out, so to fix them in place, spray them with hair lacquer before arranging them in position on your flower picture.

- *Spray finished pictures with hair lacquer to stop odd leaves and blossoms falling off.*
- *Iron skeletonized leaves carefully after gathering them — there is no need to press them.*
- *In an emergency, dry plant material in a microwave oven set on defrost. You may need to experiment first so don't use your best specimens.*
- *Swap flower stalks around if, for instance, a longer or a more curved stalk is needed.*
- *Improve a flower by sticking a small umbel or floret in its centre.*
- *Highlight a dark flower by sticking it over a larger paler flower, or by gluing small contrasting florets around the edges of the petals.*
- *Pare clumsy stalks with sharp nail scissors to make them more aesthetic.*
- *Iron out creases in petals and leaves with a cool iron.*
- *Decorate the centres of flowers with small beads or sequins for a glittering, theatrical effect.*
- *If you are short of skeletonized leaves, spray fine veiling with paint and use it as a background.*
- *Add a touch of paint to translucent flowers, such as snowdrops, to enhance their appearance.*

- *Iron mature grass heads, ferns and bracken fronds between two sheets of paper instead of pressing them.*
- *Press and dry fresh leaves by ironing with a cool iron.*
- *Cut plant material into the shape of bows to decorate bouquet pictures.*
- *Use the reverse side of a leaf if it is prettier than the right side.*
- *Use tweezers rather than forceps to handle tiny beads unless you want someone on the other side of the room to catch them!*
- *Reconstruct damaged flowers by gluing the best petals into a flower shape on a small circle of paper.*
- *Trim flowers and foliage if they are too large for your picture.*
- *Spray volatile seedheads with hair lacquer to stop the seeds falling out.*
- *Before pressing strawberries, cut them in half lengthways and remove some of the soft centre. Then pack the back of the fruit with tissues.*
- *Cut out varying shapes of skeletonized leaves by using one leaf as a template, placing it over a larger leaf, and cutting around it.*
- *When the picture is finished, stand it on its end and tap it sharply on a flat surface to remove odd fragments of plant material.*

Re-building flowers

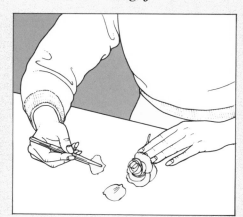

Paring clumsy stalks

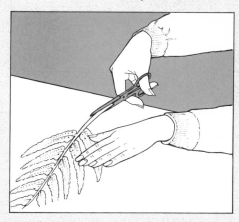

Ironing leaves

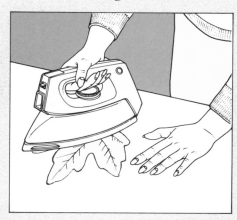

Damaged flower-heads need not be discarded. Glue new, undamaged petals in place of damaged ones. You can even build complete flower-heads using leftover petals. Glue them in a flower shape on a circle of paper.

If a stalk looks too thick and clumsy, you can pare it down so that it looks more elegant. Hold the frond flat on a table with one hand and carefully cut along the length of the stem using a pair of sharp nail scissors or a scalpel.

If you have run out of pressed leaves, iron fresh leaves carefully with a cool iron. You can also do this with ferns and bracken fronds. Be careful, however, that you don't scorch the leaves in the process. There may be some colour change.

~Making Pot Pourri~

Pot pourri is a mixture of sweet smelling leaves, flowers, spices, seeds, roots and distilled essential oils, which you can fill your sachets and pillows with (see pages 88 and 92). It is easy to make and I think a very tranquil pursuit. Many of the plants used can be grown in your garden. Roses, lilacs, lavenders, pinks, hyacinths, lilies-of-the-valley, violets, wallflowers and many more are the flowers we usually associate with perfume, but there are other plants that provide subtle fragrances, such as myrtle, geranium, daisy bush, bergamot, sage, savory, thyme, dittany, St John's-wort, angelica and sweet cicely. Any scented plant material can be gathered, dried and added to your stock pot of ingredients, including slivers of orange, lemon, lime and tangerine rind. Brightly coloured flowers and petals that have no perfume can be dried and added too; they will give a visual appeal to your pot pourri. Some seeds are fragrant too; add a few of these at a time to experiment with the combinations of scents.

It is best to gather the ingredients on a fine day. To dry leaves, tie small bunches of them together and hang them in a warm and airy place. Individual leaves, flowers and petals can be spread on trays and put somewhere warm to dry; be sure to turn them daily. Alternatively, hang them in net bags (the ones that hold oranges are ideal) with your bunches of leaves. Orange, lemon, lime and tangerine peel can be dried in a very cool oven. All plant materials can also be dried in a microwave oven; follow the instructions for drying herbs. Remember that the faster the material dries, the more perfume it will retain.

Fixatives & Oils

Fixatives will hold the perfume of any essential oils that are in your flowers and leaves, and any that you may add separately. They are vital if your pot pourri is to keep its perfume. You do not really want pretty pillows and sachets filled with pot pourri to smell of newly mown hay six months after making them! Fixatives also have a scent of their own that will add to the bouquet of your pot pourri. I always use cinnamon and orris root, in equal quantities, but you could use gum benzoin or others. Many are available from health food shops or perfumeries. Patchouli is another fixative; this adds depth and richness to a perfume but must be used with great care. Because I like the perfume in my products to be fairly pervading, I always add distilled essential oils. Rose and lavender are my favourites, but you should experiment with several different oils to find one you like. The perfume of your pot pourri will then be very individual.

HOW TO MAKE POT POURRI

1 Put the dried flowers, leaves and petals in a bowl. In a separate dish mix together the fixatives, such as orris root and cinnamon, with the flower oils. Add this mixture drop by drop to the dried flowers and leaves.

2 Using one hand, carefully mix the pot pourri ingredients together, taking care not to crush the fragile petals. Make sure all the dried flowers, petals and leaves are thoroughly coated with the fixatives and flower oils.

3 Transfer the pot pourri mixture into a lidded container and then put the lid on to seal the mixture. Shake the container well and then leave it for a week for the various oils and perfumes to amalgamate and mature.

Favourite Recipe

My own recipe for pot pourri is quite variable and has evolved over the years, through trial and error. However, it must be remembered that response to a scent is individual and, like a favourite fruit cake, the recipe will vary slightly according to the chef!

1 ½ teaspoons ground cinnamon
1 ½ teaspoons ground orris root
3 or 4 cloves
1 meagre drop patchouli oil
6 drops rose oil
2 drops lavender oil
4 cups dried flowers, petals and leaves

Mix together the cinnamon, orris root and the cloves in a bowl. Add the patchouli oil and the rose and lavender oils. Mix well together and then add slowly to the dried flowers, petals and leaves, making sure all the ingredients are thoroughly amalgamated. Put the mixture in a sealed container, shake well and then leave it for at least a week.

This can start off your stock pot of pot pourri which you can add to as more ingredients become available. Every so often, top up the fixatives and oils. I always have a container of pot pourri "on the go", the perfume of which varies depending on the dried flowers added.

Pot pourri container
Victorian pot pourri containers with their ornate decoration make a charming feature in a room, while the holes in the lid allow the scent of the pot pourri to pervade the air.

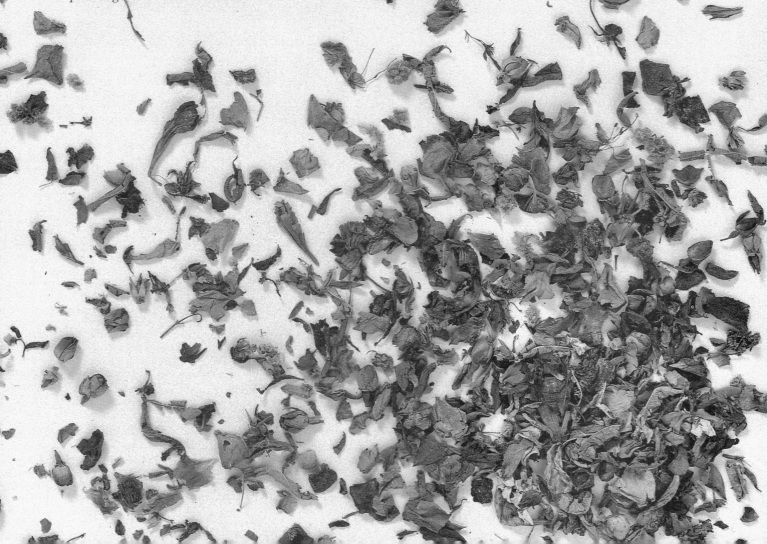

~*Fabric Dyeing*~

As I often use fabrics in my work, both as backgrounds to my flower pictures, and for making perfumed cushions and sachets (see pages 88 and 92) it did not take me long to discover the possibilities of dyeing fabric. Dyeing is an ancient and important craft. You have only to look at antique Persian carpets (which are often on show in museums) to see the inherent beauty of plant dyes. Many of these old carpets depicted gardens and from them you can see the designs of the ancient walled gardens of Persia; many of the plants in these gardens must have been used to dye the silks of the carpets.

Dye Plants

There are many plants, both wild and cultivated, that will render a dye you can use. Marigolds and nasturtiums, both commonly grown in gardens, produce rich orange and yellow dyes, while the crushed leaves of woad yield a deep blue dye. For varying shades of green, try nettles, dog's mercury and lily-of-the-valley leaves; for hues of yellow, try the leaves and stems of lady's bedstraw, the flower-heads of meadowsweet and pieces of lichen. And for a strong red colour, use the roots of alkanet, that lovely flower of the hedgerows with its blue flower-head that may be pale or dark blue in colour. Then, of course, there are all kinds of berries that you can use in dyeing: blackberries and elderberries for a soft pinkish-purple dye and sloe berries for a golden beige colour.

Even if you live in the centre of town, you can still participate in this homespun pursuit. Instead of using wild flowers and plants, if they are hard to come by, why not try exotic spices, such as saffron and turmeric, which yield lovely rich gold and yellow dyes, giving a suggestion of the mysterious East. More down to earth, perhaps, are tea and coffee which yield a rose-tan dye, onion skins which produce a soft burnt orange colour, and cochineal food colouring for a soft pale pink. You could experiment with all sorts of plants and vegetables and you might be pleasantly surprised at the results.

I am by no means an expert or informed dyer but I am enthusiastic when I feel it is a means to an end as far as

---

HOW TO DYE FABRIC

1 Wash and rinse the fabric. Put ¼oz soda crystals *or* 1½ teaspoons of salt *or* 1½ teaspoons of bicarbonate of soda (all mordants) in an enamel or steel saucepan. Fill the pan three-quarters full with water and bring it to the boil. Then add the fabric and boil (cotton or linen) or simmer (silk) for one hour. Remove the pan from the heat and leave the fabric to cool in the pan overnight. The fabric is now mordanted.

2 Remove the fabric from the pan and refill it three-quarters full with fresh water. If you are using flowers, leaves or berries for dyeing, insert them in a nylon stocking, knot the end, and immerse the stocking in the water. Dyes such as saffron and turmeric can be added straight to the pan; tea and coffee can remain in their bags. Bring the water to the boil and allow it to simmer for one hour to release the dye.

3 Slowly immerse the mordanted fabric in the dye pan, taking care not to splash or scald yourself. There is no need to remove any of the dye plants or materials from the pan as more colour might still be released. Should the dye appear too pale, add an extra ½ teaspoon of mordant — soda crystals, salt or bicarbonate of soda — to the pan. Swish the fabric around and bring the water to the boil (cotton or linen) or simmering point (silk).

my craft is concerned. I don't follow any textbook instructions when dyeing fabric, but the resulting colours have intrinsic charm, are usually quite pale and no two colours are ever quite the same! As I use a relatively small container in which to dye my fabric, I can only dye small amounts of fabric at a time. So I usually end up with a selection of materials in varying depths of colour. But that is what I like. Little sachets and bags look quite individual when made from these fabrics. I have also dyed lace to make it look antique, particularly if I've been using a modern white cotton lace, or even old lace that I have washed white. If you are edging a flower sampler or a formal romantic garland with lace, it is essential that the colour of the lace is a discreet ecru, so as to give the right feel to the picture. Tea and coffee are the best dyes for this.

Dyeing Preparation

I only dye natural fabrics such as cotton, linen and silk, as these are the only fabrics I use in my work. Before dyeing the fabric, make sure it is either its natural colour, or white. Any coloured fabric should be bleached first.

As well as the dye plant or substance, you will need a mordant, which makes the fabric more receptive to the dye. You can buy chemical mordants, but I only use mordants that I have in the house, such as soda crystals, bicarbonate of soda or salt.

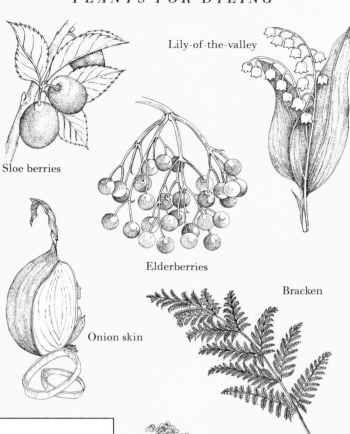

PLANTS FOR DYEING

Sloe berries

Lily-of-the-valley

Elderberries

Onion skin

Bracken

Lichen

Marigold

Moss

4 To ensure that the fabric is dyed evenly, stir it frequently around the pan, using wooden tongs. Keep checking the colour of the fabric to see whether the dye is taking. If you want a fairly pale colour, as I usually do, then the dyeing may only take half an hour; if you want a darker shade, this will take longer but you should play it by ear. Bear in mind that your fabric will be a slightly lighter colour when it is dry.

5 When the desired intensity of colour is reached, remove the dye pan from the heat. Lift the fabric out of the pan, using wooden tongs, and rinse it several times in warm water. Hang it out to dry, then iron it carefully when it is still damp. The dyed fabric can now be used for making a wide variety of things, such as perfumed sachets, or lace pillows, or for using as a background to your flower pictures.

~ *Picture Framing* ~

Whether your picture is bold and colourful, or pale and pretty, a picture frame will enhance the impact your picture has and give it some protection at the same time. You can frame your pictures with or without mounts, but the advantage of using a mount is that it gives the picture an extra surround, separating it from the frame, and allowing the picture to be seen more clearly.

There are several options available to you when it comes to obtaining a frame; you can make one yourself, have one made professionally, or buy a ready-made frame. Whatever you choose, your frame will need to be fairly deep to accommodate the texture of your pressed flower material. You may have to insert a thin fillet of wood between the glass and the picture or mount to add depth.

Making a Frame

Making your own frame requires a certain amount of skill and practice. First, using a mitre cutter, cut four pieces of wood moulding, the shortest sides equal to the length of the picture or mount edges. Glue the four cut

edges of the frame together into a rectangular shape, clamping each corner in a corner clamp. Using a nail punch, drive pins into the wood to secure the corners. Insert glass, mount, picture, backing and then hardboard into the frame and then secure the hardboard with pins and gummed paper.

Buying a Frame

There is quite an art in selecting the right kind of frame and mount and it is a good idea to experiment with different ones. A good professional framer can offer advice although your own taste will ultimately dictate what you choose. To judge the effect of the frame, stand well back from your picture, about 2 metres (6 feet) away. Remember that the most important thing is the dominance of your picture and its composition. I prefer discreet frames as I feel that pressed flower pictures should not be overpowered.

I rarely buy the more elaborate and expensive picture frames. Simple pine frames, with their natural feel make

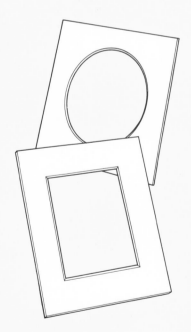

Cutting out a mount

Cutting a mount with a bevelled edge requires some practice for the result to look clean and neat. Use a heavy metal ruler and a mount cutter or a sharp knife. Mark the lines to be cut on the reverse

side of the card mount. Hold the ruler down flat along the marked line and then, holding the mount cutter flat, or a knife at a slant, carefully draw it along the ruler towards you.

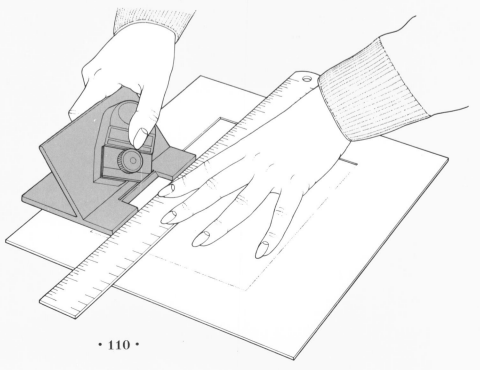

Choice of mounts

Choose your mount to complement your picture. Rectangular mounts create a strong impression, whereas oval mounts are less stern and are ideal for soft and romantic compositions.

ideal surrounds to most pressed flower pictures and vegetable collages. To make them more glossy, try waxing them with a gold or silver wax polish. You can also paint pine frames in bright and cheerful colours. I tend to paint my frames either a colour that echoes that of the mount, or white. A rich and colourful collage, mounted on hand-made white paper, can look stunning surrounded by a simple white frame. It is best to use a spray paint when painting your frames as this will give a more professional finish.

You can also get simple metal frames which have a cool, modern image. These are suitable for abstract collages and botanical compositions. Wood veneer frames in oak and yew are also available. They succeed in having an air of luxury whilst still retaining their natural feel.

Renovating Old Frames

A cheap way of obtaining unusual picture frames is to rummage around junk and antique shops for old or discarded frames. Really beautiful antique frames are now hard to find and in any case might be too heavy and elaborate for a pressed flower picture. However, some of the less expensive old wooden frames can look charming; their shapes have something that their modern counterparts lack. Try stripping them and you may find lovely mellow pine bases. Damaged gesso frames can be scraped and cleaned or cut down to make smaller frames. With imagination, stripper, wax polish and paint you can transform ugly plasterwork frames into simple and cheerful surrounds for your pictures. Stamped tin frames

Stamped tin frame
An old-fashioned tin frame,
stamped with a floral design, makes
an ideal surround for a pressed flower picture.

are cheap to buy and always look delightful surrounding flower pictures. If you are lucky you may find old wooden liners (a border within the frame). I love them as they immediately add a feeling of nostalgia, entirely in keeping with my flower pictures.

Inserting a fillet of wood

If your picture frame is not very deep, the textured plant material in the picture may be squashed against the glass of the frame. To prevent this, place four thin strips of wood inside the frame, after inserting the glass and before the picture is put in. These fillets create a ledge for the picture to rest on, separating it from the glass.

Repainting an old frame

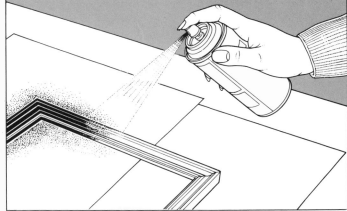

To make an old frame presentable, first remove any old paint and varnish with paint stripper. Then sandpaper the frame so that the surface is smooth, and clean it with a soft damp cloth. Repaint the frame with spray paint, rather than using a paintbrush, as this gives a smooth finish. Add further coats, if required.

~ *Planning Your Garden* ~

Wherever you live and whatever your garden is like, you will probably already be growing plants that are suitable for pressing. However, if you are planning to do a lot of flower pressing, it might be a good idea to devote your garden, or part of it, to growing flowers that lend themselves well to this treatment. The greater your choice of flowers to press, the greater scope you will have when making your flower pictures.

Our relatively mild and wet climate enables us to grow many hardy plants from all over the world and, in some parts of the country, very tender plants will survive. Add to this the richness of our native flora, found in woodlands, hedgerows and meadows, and you will be spoilt for choice when deciding what to grow in your garden.

Cottage-Garden Style

My own garden is wild, informal, probably over-planted and a mixture of both cultivated and wild plants. I love abundance in a garden, where everything intermingles, and where plants flop over the edges of flowerbeds and seed themselves everywhere. I let the aristocratic mix with the humble: beautiful Tibetan poppies hobnob with black-veined dock; a jumble of old roses grows with columbines and sweet-smelling dame's-violet; while carpets of common dog-violet intermingle with alpine strawberries along my garden path.

Lush and informal wild gardens can be created on any scale, from a large and rambling back garden, to a tiny pocket handkerchief-sized front garden. With the exception of self-perpetuating annuals it is best to grow perennial plants, both to save yourself time and to establish rambling growth in your garden. In small areas there will be no room for a lawn, but remember to allow space for meandering paths or stepping stones. For a feeling of abundance, plants should jostle for space rather than follow a contrived planting scheme. Plant tall specimens in the foreground as well as in the background and then surround them in turn with ground-hugging plants. Plant climbers so that they scramble not only up and over walls and trees, but also through shrubs.

Plants to Grow

Many plants, such as forget-me-nots, columbines, primroses, Welsh poppies, quaking-grass, bugle and violets will seed themselves liberally and thus spread quickly. Of course some must be thinned out every so often but don't be too harsh. Let the garden have an air of unplanned profusion, and allow seedlings to grow in the chinks and crevices of walls, rockeries and paths in which they have chosen to germinate. Our gravel drive is a patchwork of primroses in April and, yes, they *do* get driven over and trodden upon, but it really doesn't seem to worry them. One year a beautiful red monkey musk even seeded itself in the gutters of our barn and bloomed profusely throughout the summer!

When planning your garden, think about the resulting colour associations of your plants. If you like a particular colour combination that unexpectedly evolves in your garden, you can recreate this in your flower pictures.

If you have any shady, damp areas in your garden, a lovely wild plant you can grow is hemlock water-dropwort. Grow it with angelica and sweet cicely and you will have an ample supply of umbels and little florets for pressing. Other pretty wild plants include herb-robert, which will grow happily almost anywhere and rosebay willowherb, which was once cultivated in cottage gardens. This makes a striking garden plant and it presses wonderfully. If at all possible try to obtain the white variety as well as the more common magenta, as the two grow together very well. I also love the green panicles of wild hop and my plant makes an annual pilgrimage up an unsightly telegraph pole. Pressed when young they can be used to edge or soften a wildflower collage. Even common yellow ragwort looks lovely when pressed and I grow this (with some reluctance, I must admit) on our terrace. I have no hesitation growing celandines, however. They grow with such abundance in a shady patch of our lawn that I don't think any grass has survived, but we do have a wonderful lake of yellow and green in spring.

Cultivating Your Garden

Wild gardens, and even cottage gardens, are not quite as easy to cultivate as they sound. Initially there is a lot of planting and weeding to be done for you will have many undesirable inhabitants. Just turning the soil in my garden unleashes armies of dock seedlings! However, you can gain a lot of satisfaction in working hard at creating your own tamed wilderness. To encourage and maintain lush growth the soil must be fairly rich and each year a good organic mulch should be spread around. I use well-rotted horse manure, but you could use cow manure or peat and a good organic fertilizer.

Simple Garden Plan

Illustrated opposite is a garden plan suitable for a front garden or small back garden. It contains most of the essential plants you will need for pressing and follows the relaxed and rambling garden style that I love. Remember that the more plants you can grow, the better choice you will have when making your flower pictures.

SIMPLE GARDEN PLAN

Pathway of crushed bark

Low brick wall

Garden gate

Alchemilla mollis
Lady's-mantle

Garden fence

Hedera helix
'Goldheart' Ivy

Astilbe × arendsii

Astilbe × arendsii

Hedera helix
Ivy

Rosa farreri persetosa
Threepenny-bit rose

Geranium endressii
Crane's-bill

Delphinium spp.
Larkspur

Wooden pergola

Eryngium giganteum

Clematis recta

Salvia officinalis
Sage

Geum chiloense
Avens

Anthriscus sylvestris
Cow parsley

Knautia arvensis
Field scabious

Veronica virginica
Speedwell

Geranium pratense
Meadow crane's-bill

Delphinium spp.
Larkspur

Anthriscus sylvestris
Cow parsley

Low brick wall

Anaphalis yedoensis
Everlasting

Astrantia maxima

Potentilla
'Gibson's Scarlet'

Rosa 'Vilchenblau'

Rosa moyesii 'Geranium'

Humulus lupulus aurea
Golden hops

Geum chiloense
Avens

Crocosmia crocosmiiflora

Potentilla fruticosa

Lysimachia ephemerum
Loosestrife

Anemone japonica
Japanese anemone

Epimedium × rubrum
Barrenwort

Crocosmia crocosmiiflora

Sanguisorba tenuifolia
Burnet

Tellima grandiflora

Rosa 'Scarlet Fire'

Pulmonaria saccharata
Lungwort

Fragaria spp.
Alpine strawberry

Polystichum aculeatum
Hard shield fern

Potentilla 'Red Ace'

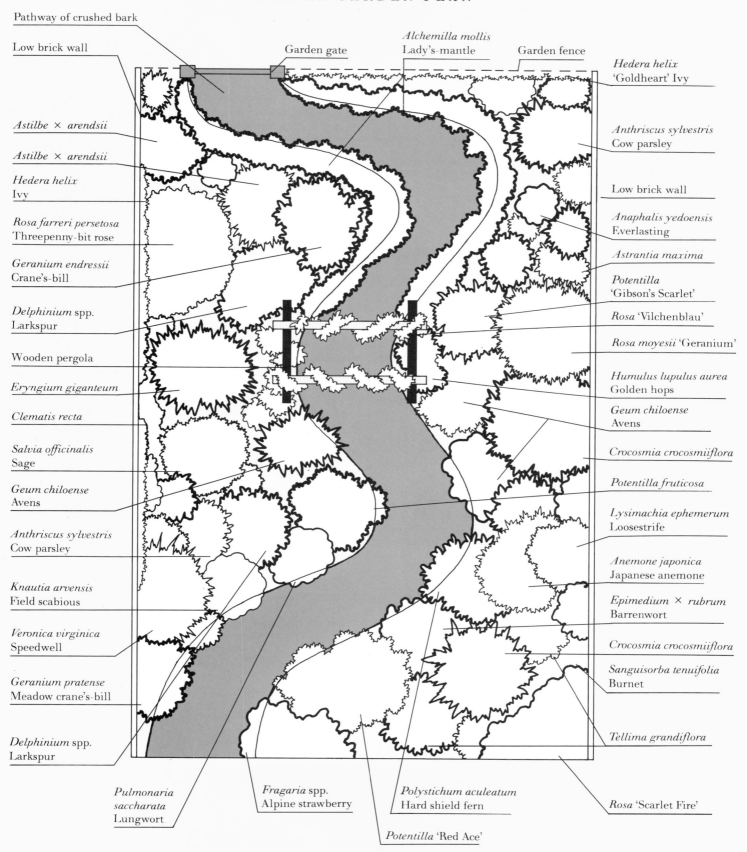

~*Balcony Garden*~

If you live in a city and only have a balcony or courtyard garden, there is no reason why you shouldn't grow both wild and cultivated flowers for pressing. In just a few square metres you could create a little garden of great variety and interest and one that would supply you with enough plant material to start you on the road to making pressed flower pictures!

With care and attention many plants can be grown in containers of some sort or other and there is a wide choice of different containers available in wood, earthenware or plastic: troughs, tubs, window boxes, wall boxes, hanging baskets, pots or barrels, to name just a few.

Tubs and Pots

Old porcelain sinks are a good idea. They are usually quite deep, allowing the more rampant plants space to scramble around, and those plants with deep, questing roots the depth to grow with freedom. Window boxes, wall boxes and hanging baskets have the advantage of giving you more growing area on the ground. Half-barrels are wonderful — in them you can cultivate a complete little garden. If you look around there are many other possibilities in the world of containers but don't be restricted by convention; what could look lovelier than a discarded porcelain lavatory pan burgeoning with ivies, ferns, fuchsias and sweet cicely!

Mix wild flowers with garden varieties in your pots for they can look delightful growing together. For an air of profusion, cram all your troughs, tubs, pots and containers together and grow your flowers cheek by jowl. Try to grow as wide a selection as possible of blossoms, umbels, sprays and spiky plants to give you greater choice when assembling your flower collages.

To give your plants a flying start it is a good idea to use good potting compost. Either buy the appropriate ready-mixed compost from your local garden centre or, better still, mix some yourself. The proportions I use are 2 parts loam or compost, 1 part top grade peat or leafmould, and 1 part coarse sand or grit. Before you fill your containers with compost, make sure that they have drainage holes and a layer of stones, or broken crocks at the bottom. This will prevent your compost from turning sour. Remember to water your containers regularly as the compost will dry out very quickly. For really lush growth give your plants foliar feeds during the growing season.

Don't forget, however, if you wish to add more flowers to your stock for pressing, even in cities, weeds such as dandelions and daisies grow in the most unlikely nooks and crannies. You could also buy a few fresh or dried flowers to press to supplement your stock.

Plants for Pressing

I have listed below the flowers that you can grow in containers for pressing. (Suppliers of wild flowers and seeds are listed at the back of the book.) I have made suggestions as to which type of container would best fulfil the needs of these plants but plants do, of course, spread and increase and every once in a while even a small plant will outgrow its container and must either be divided or be transplanted into a larger pot.

TUBS
Achillea millefolium Yarrow
Alchemilla mollis Lady's-mantle
Anemone japonica Japanese anemone
Anthriscus sylvestris Cow parsley
Astrantia spp.
Chamerion angustifolium
   Rosebay willowherb
Clematis recta
Fuchsia magellanica
Geranium pratense Meadow crane's-bill
Humulus lupulus aurea Golden hops
Myrica gale Myrtle
Myrrhis odorata Sweet cicely
Rosa moyesii 'Geranium'
Bulbs
Anemone spp.
Colchicum spp. Crocus
Galanthus nivalis Snowdrop
Muscari spp. Grape hyacinth

Herbs
Borago officinalis Borage
Cryptogramma spp. Parsley
Mentha spp. Ginger mint
Origanum spp. Marjoram
Rosmarinus spp. Rosemary
Salvia spp. Sage
Thymus spp. Thyme

WINDOW & WALL BOXES
Anchusa capensis Alkanet
Anthemis spp.
   Chamomile (double and single)
Bellis perennis 'Pomponette' Daisy
Calendula spp. Marigold
Delphinium spp. Larkspur
Eschscholzia spp. Californian poppy
Fragaria spp. Alpine strawberry
Linaria spp. Toadflax
Lobelia spp.

Myosotis spp. Forget-me-not
Nigella spp. Love-in-a-mist
Scabiosa atropurpurea Scabious
Viola spp. Pansy

POTS
Alchemilla mollis Lady's-mantle
Anthemis spp. Chamomile
Astrantia spp.
Borago officinalis Borage
Daucus carota gummifer Sea carrot
Geum chiloense Avens
Hedera spp. Ivy
Mentha spp. Ginger mint
Origanum spp. Marjoram
Potentilla spp.
Rosa chinensis minima Fairy rose
Tanacetum parthenium Feverfew
Thymus spp. Thyme
Veronica virginica Speedwell

SIMPLE BALCONY GARDEN PLAN

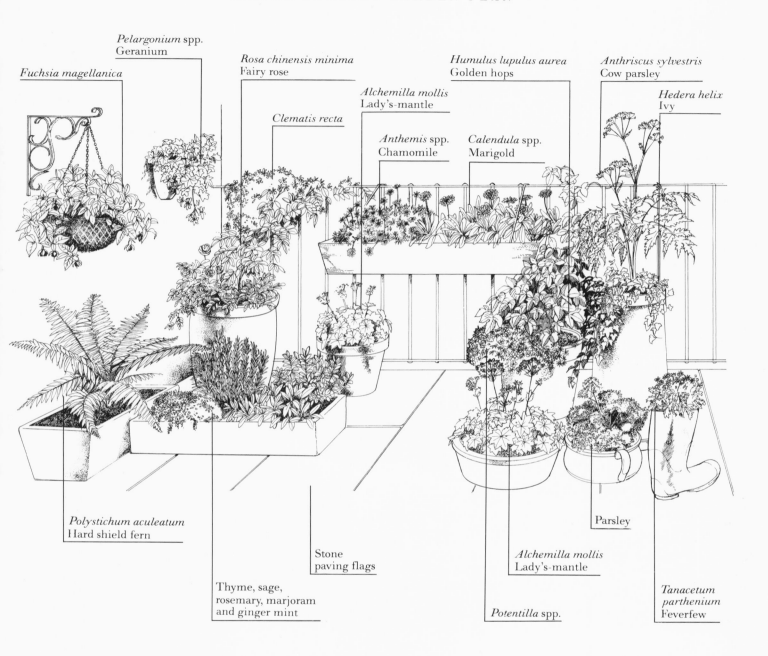

Fuchsia magellanica

Pelargonium spp.
Geranium

Rosa chinensis minima
Fairy rose

Clematis recta

Alchemilla mollis
Lady's-mantle

Anthemis spp.
Chamomile

Calendula spp.
Marigold

Humulus lupulus aurea
Golden hops

Anthriscus sylvestris
Cow parsley

Hedera helix
Ivy

Polystichum aculeatum
Hard shield fern

Stone
paving flags

Thyme, sage,
rosemary, marjoram
and ginger mint

Alchemilla mollis
Lady's-mantle

Parsley

Potentilla spp.

*Tanacetum
parthenium*
Feverfew

A Selection of Terracotta Pots

Conservation of Wild Flowers

The richness of our flora, encouraged by our wet climatic conditions, is one of the most varied in the world. However, modern methods of farming and forestry, the demolition of our hedgerows, the draining of our fens and marshes and the ploughing of our ancient meadows, have destroyed the habitats of many of our beautiful native plants and the very essence of our countryside is disappearing. It is up to us to do something about it and with this in mind I would recommend that everyone thinks carefully before picking any wild flowers.

Many rare wild flowers are now, thankfully, protected by law and must not be picked or uprooted (see the Schedule of Protected Plants below). The penalty is a fine of up to £500 for each plant. This is at least a start in protecting what remains but we should still be careful and sensible nevertheless. Common sense will tell you that it is quite permissible to pick dandelions, daisies, docks and many other common weeds, but even these only in moderation. Always leave some flowers behind to set seed, never pick flowers from a plant that has no companions and pick no more than you really need. Respect our mosses and lichens and if possible encourage them to grow in your own garden. Try to grow your own wild flowers in your garden, particularly the more unusual ones (see page 120 for suppliers of wildflower seeds and plants) and pass on spare seedlings to your friends and neighbours. We must all play our part in the conservation of our wonderful plant life.

SCHEDULE OF PROTECTED PLANTS

Common name	Scientific name	Common name	Scientific name
Adder's-tongue spearwort	Ranunculus ophioglossifolius	Norwegian sandwort	Arenaria norvegica
Alpine catchfly	Lychnis alpina	Oblong woodsia	Woodsia ilvensis
Alpine gentian	Gentiana nivalis	Oxtongue broomrape	Orobanche loricata
Alpine sow-thistle	Cicerbita alpina	Perennial knawel	Scleranthus perennis
Alpine woodsia	Woodsia alpina	Plymouth pear	Pyrus cordata
Bedstraw broomrape	Orobanche caryophyllacea	Purple spurge	Euphorbia peplis
Blue heath	Phyllodoce caerulea	Red helleborine	Cephalanthera rubra
Brown galingale	Cyperus fuscus	Ribbon-leaved water-plantain	Alisma gramineum
Cheddar pink	Dianthus gratianopolitanus	Rock cinquefoil	Potentilla rupestris
Childling pink	Petrorhagia nanteuilii	Rock sea-lavender	Limonium paradoxum
Diapensia	Diapensia lapponica	(two rare species)	Limonium recurvum
Dickie's bladder-fern	Cystopteris dickieana	Rough marsh-mallow	Althaea hirsuta
Downy woundwort	Stachys germanica	Round-headed leek	Allium sphaerocephalon
Drooping saxifrage	Saxifraga cernua	Sea knotgrass	Polygonum maritimum
Early spider-orchid	Ophrys sphegodes	Sickle-leaved hare's-ear	Bupleurum falcatum
Fen orchid	Liparis loeselii	Small Alison	Alyssum alyssoides
Fen violet	Viola persicifolia	Small hare's-ear	Bupleurum baldense
Field cow-wheat	Melampyrum arvense	Snowdon lily	Lloydia serotina
Field eryngo	Eryngium campestre	Spiked speedwell	Veronica spicata
Field wormwood	Artemisia campestris	Spring gentian	Gentiana verna
Ghost orchid	Epipogium aphyllum	Starfruit	Damasonium alisma
Greater yellow-rattle	Rhinanthus serotinus	Starved wood-sedge	Carex depauperata
Jersey cudweed	Gnaphalium luteoalbum	Teesdale sandwort	Minuartia stricta
Killarney fern	Trichomanes speciosum	Thistle broomrape	Orobanche reticulata
Lady's-slipper	Cypripedium calceolus	Triangular club-rush	Scirpus triquetrus
Late spider-orchid	Ophrys fuciflora	Tufted saxifrage	Saxifraga cespitosa
Least lettuce	Lactuca saligna	Water germander	Teucrium scordium
Limestone woundwort	Stachys alpina	Whorled solomon's-seal	Polygonatum verticillatum
Lizard orchid	Himantoglossum hircinum	Wild cotoneaster	Cotoneaster integerrimus
Military orchid	Orchis militaris	Wild gladiolus	Gladiolus illyricus
Monkey orchid	Orchis simia	Wood calamint	Calamintha sylvatica

Index

Page numbers in italic refer to illustrations and captions

Suppliers

Equipment Suppliers

Dryad
P.O. Box 38
Leicester LE1 9BU
Flower presses, card and ancillary items.
Write for a list of stockists in your area

Falkiner Fine Papers
76 Southampton Row
London WC1B 4AR
Hand-made paper, pens and inks

A.L. Hill, City Picture Frames
Carvedras
George Street
Truro
Cornwall
Mounts and frames

Malins Hall Gallery
17a High Street
Falmouth
Cornwall
Frames, mounts and artists' materials

The Two Rivers Paper Company
Rosebank Mill
Stubbins
Nr Bury
Lancashire
Hand-made paper

Plant Suppliers

Penny Black
Treskewes Cottage
Trewithen Moor
Stithians
Truro
Cornwall
Old-fashioned primroses and plants for the damp garden

John Chambers
15 Westleigh Road
Barton Seagrave
Kettering
Northamptonshire NN15 5AJ
Wildflower bulbs and plants

Landlife Wild Flowers Ltd
The Old Police Station
Lark Lane
Liverpool L17 8UU
Wildflower plants and seeds

Suffolk Herbs Ltd
Sawyer's Farm
Little Cornard
Sudbury
Suffolk CO10 0NY
Wildflower plants and seeds

Acknowledgments

Author's acknowledgments
I would like to thank all those at Dorling Kindersley who have made this book possible: Fiona Macmillan for her creative help and unfailing encouragement; Heather Dewhurst for understanding the essence of my message when editing; and David Lamb, Jackie Douglas and Roger Bristow, all of whom played their part. I would also like to thank Geoff Dann for his photographs and for taking such a constructive interest in the project. To *Country Living* magazine I extend a special thank you, for without its feature article there would never have been the possibility of a book in the first place. Last, but by no means least, I would like to thank my husband, Bob, who has patiently listened to all my problems and enthusiastically joined me on many a wild goose chase!

Dorling Kindersley would like to thank the following for their help in producing this book: Richard Bird, Kate Grant and Suzanna Longley.

Photographic credits
All photography by Geoff Dann except for:
p.8 (top) Jacqui Hurst.

Illustrators
David Ashby, Vana Haggerty, Haywood Art Group.